RUNNING IN PLACE

ALSO BY NICHOLAS DELBANCO:

The Beaux Arts Trio
About My Table & Other Stories
Group Portrait: Conrad, Crane, Ford, James, and Wells
Stillness
Sherbrookes
Possession
Small Rain
Fathering
In the Middle Distance
News
Consider Sappho Burning
Grasse 3/23/66
The Martlet's Tale

Nicholas Delbanco

RUNNING IN PLACE:

Scenes from the
South of France

THE ATLANTIC MONTHLY PRESS
NEW YORK
•

Published simultaneously in Canada
Printed in the United States of America
FIRST EDITION

Library of Congress Cataloging-in-Publication Data
Delbanco, Nicholas.
Running in place : scenes from the south of France / Nicholas
Delbanco.—1st ed.
ISBN 0-87113-320-2
I. Title.
PS3554.E442R86   1989   813'.54—dc19   88-27031

The Atlantic Monthly Press
19 Union Square West
New York, NY 10003

FIRST PRINTING

For Elena, Francesca, Andrea:
fellow travelers.

There is an art of the future, and it is going to be so lovely and so young that even if we give up our youth for it we must gain by it in serenity. Perhaps it is very silly to write all this, but I feel it so; it seems to me that, like me, you have been suffering to see your youth pass like a drift of smoke, but if it springs up again and comes to life in what you do, nothing has been lost, and the power to work is another youth.

VINCENT VAN GOGH, letter to his brother Theo, 1886

NOTE

The author wishes to thank the Michigan Council for the Arts and the Graduate School of the University of Michigan Rackham Faculty Grants Award Program. They supported this enterprise generously indeed, and I am grateful to both. Thanks also to the Corporation of Yaddo, for their welcome and welcoming space.

The young man's study is the self. Mine was, at any rate. In the early years here chronicled, I took parental help—the whole network of adult attention—for granted. Yet the support of parents should not go unacknowledged; I remain in their debt to this day.

Some of the names have been changed. This is not to protect the innocent, since all of us were innocents abroad. But the less public people deserve to have their privacy respected, and the famous names seem less distracting when dropped. I could not bring myself, however, to disguise James Baldwin; his was a lifelong insistence on the role of truthful witness. I was not in France when he died. His death in December of 1987 is therefore not part of this narrative. Yet it is an enduring loss—as were earlier, and lastingly, the deaths of my mother and the man I here call

Alexander Bechstein. To them—and to my father, who continues to this day his fond bemused indulgence—go my enduring thanks.

I

✻

1987

A man jumped into my wife's tub while she was taking a bath. This happened in Paris, in our hotel, at seven o'clock in the morning. It was the start of July. The hotel was small, family-style, and being painted; there was scaffolding outside. We had a corner room, however, and the window in the bathroom gave on air. Elena left this window open, locked the door—which otherwise would not stay shut—ran a bubble bath, and lay down to luxuriate. I read in the next room.

Two shoeless feet swung through the window's top, and she shouted, "No. I'm in the bath!" They continued to swing there—blue pants and black socks. She thought perhaps it was a workman who had lost his footing and was trying to gain purchase on the ledge. A drop would have been murderous; she could not slam the window on his feet. Also, she was naked, covered in bubbles, and flustered; he jackknifed through and fell into the tub.

I had heard the shouting, but the bathroom door was locked. He was saying "Sorry, sorry, sorry" by the time she reached to open it, and he kept on saying "Sorry!" as I threw him out. He was fully dressed if shoeless, maybe thirty years old, brown-haired and soaked and horrified. I had not seen strangers in my wife's bathtub before, and I

3

was not gentle. He fell into the hall. I called the concierge to say that a wet man with no shoes was coming down the staircase, and they should stop and question him. The first reaction—the quintessential French response—was, "I assure you, sir, he does not work for us."

Then there was shouting, the excited noise of capture, the man still saying "Sorry!" as he staggered to the lobby. I learned his story later, when they had let him go. He had stolen nothing; he was not a workman, not a guest. He had stayed in the hotel for a week, two weeks earlier; his lover—a gentleman from somewhere north, the concierge assured me, a stranger—had gone. This one was not a favorite of the chambermaids, you understand, monsieur. He never left the room. He lay in bed all day and ate his food there and was quiet enough and the bill had been paid, but still there was something peculiar; he did not leave willingly that first time he departed. *Enfin,* this morning he had returned. They assured him his friend had checked out. He said, "All right, I'll wait a little," and sat in the lobby. They did not make him welcome, but he had the right to sit.

Through all of this the manager was gauging me, wondering how much to confide, how much I might protest. When I told him my wife was unharmed, he decided to tell me the rest: how this poor madman, *ce fou,* had made his way to the basement and taken the elevator up while no one noticed—the manager spread his hands, *dommage*—and knocked on his old door, the one above the room we occupied, 22 not 12, not believing, apparently, that his lover had left. The door was opened by a couple expecting breakfast, and he pushed his way through and did not find his friend and, crazed, jumped out of the window to what was certain death. But he must have changed his mind and jumped back in the floor below into—he shrugged, not yet risking a wink—your wife's bath. The carpet was soaked. Also, he marred the fresh exterior paint. There were fingerprints all down the stairwell. "And the shoes?" I asked. "Why wasn't he wearing shoes?" "Oh, he left them in the hallway when he knocked on 22, he believed he could surprise the Swede inside." But he did not find his lover and could only repeat the word "sorry"—eyes like pinwheels, hair in suds.

It *was* a sorry history, and the manager hoped I would not blame them and that we would return. I assured him we had no ill feelings, this would make a story some-day. He said, "You're kind to understand," and sent a second breakfast upstairs to Elena. But I have been haunted, lately, by that leap—the split-second reversal of purpose, the window providentially unlocked. And then the comic denouement, the woman in bubbles, the outraged husband, the apparatus of farce.

Yet one man's farce is another man's dead earnest; it de-pends on point of view. And I find myself watching this trip from a shifting, doubling vantage, through just such a set of bifocals. We plan a sentimental journey to our early haunts. Elena and I have been married sixteen years; it is time to show our daughters where we cavorted when young. We want to see collectively what we once saw alone. It is to be, I tell myself, a chance to travel with our daughters before we drift apart, a chance to share our past with them before it proves irrecoverable.

We are driving from the valley of the Loire to the Dordogne. The distance is not great, but the roads are clotted with cars. We have rented a house sight unseen. Though journey's end will be Provence—that wedge of France above the sea—the trip south feels leisurely. A plumb line dropped from Paris would have taken us much nearer our prospective home. My family voted for speed. Had we used the *autoroute,* we might have reached Lourmarin in a day. I insisted on this detour, since I want to see Lascaux.

June was cold and rainy, but July has come in with a vengeance. The day is windless, cloudless, hot. We rented a car in Paris, a Citroën BX16RS Station Wagon. "The roomiest and most comfortable station wagon in its class," the agency proclaimed. We needed space; the four of us have a good deal of luggage, and our younger daughter, Andrea, grows carsick when crammed in. At nine years old, she distrusts travel and needs to be precise. "How long will it take us; when will we get there?" she asks. That we have no accurate answer makes her fearful; it's better to name a target time than to admit uncertainty. So I say, "Four o'clock." This also has its pitfalls; she groans at the number of hours entailed. She says, "It's too long, Daddy. Way too long." But the risk of being late—of arriving at four-thirty —is greater, since she will say, at twenty to four, "Twenty more minutes, correct? You promised. You said so. You're wrong."

Her elder sister, Francesca, leavens tolerance with exasperation; thirteen, she seesaws back and forth between accomplice and judge. Were Cesca to be the jury, Andrea would have hanged. They sprawl together in the back, wearing Walkmen, trading tapes at intervals, and mouthing their separate songs. Andrea has just learned to whistle; she whistles, but not Cesca's tune. I do the driving, mostly, while Elena charts our course. She has a sense of direction keen as an animal's, and she likes reading maps. Our destination for the night is the village just beyond Lascaux, the "capital of prehistory": Les Eyzies-de-Tayac.

"What did you like best so far?"

"The Sound and Light," Andrea says.

"The one at Versailles? Or the Château de Chambord?"

I watch her in the rearview mirror. She nods.

That morning we heard a sad story. We stayed two nights in the Loire Valley in a private home with rooms for rent. "When the Socialists moved in," said the owner—a redoubtable woman in blue who kept a Gauloise on her lower lip and an eye peeled for incompetence among the staff—"when they took over, our taxes tripled, and so to make ends meet we make you welcome, yes? Here is the library, here are my books. The toilet fails to function if any sort of object is within. Your children will take chocolate for breakfast, they are proper girls. This part of the house is fifteenth century, the part where you sleep is eighteenth. Welcome. *Soyez les bienvenues.*"

There was a park at the rear of the house, a Renais-

7

sance garden in front. Dogs were not permitted in the front. The park contained impressive topiary, a formal arrangement of boxwood and elder, a cypress hedge so thick that walkways had been carved within to make a green arched maze. The garden, in contrast, was lush: grapes, artichokes, lettuce, fruit trees, and flowers in organized profusion, the gravel walkways raked. There was to have been a wedding; they had prepared all month. Their son was getting married, and they had expected three hundred guests for Saturday. But he was in the hospital with a sudden attack of what they hoped was only phlebitis, and the wedding was postponed until at least September, or perhaps cancelled, and certainly the festivities were cancelled, and nothing was as it should be. Madame was going to the hospital this afternoon; she hoped the bride-to-be would be there too. She was not sure. She doubted it. She lit a cigarette. She shook out the match and continued to shake it. The gardens, however, were just as they should be, *comme il fallait.* They were in a state of readiness; they were far more ready than her son.

We left. We made our winding way through Tours, Poitiers, Limoges, and had lunch—salads, ham, an entrecôte, cold rosé in pitchers—in a converted farm by the side of the road near Saint-Yrieix-la-Perche. There were more tractors than cars. We then lazed down to Montignac, farm country still, the fields replete with new-mown hay and signs for Lascaux II. The Walkmen were fading. They needed their batteries changed.

The story of Lascaux can be briefly told. Four boys stumbled into it on September 12, 1940, following Robot, their dog. (The dog may have been a journalist's embellishment, to lend the "human" touch; Jacques Marsal—one of the four discoverers, and now the cave's official guardian—denies there was a dog.) The boys returned next day with adequate light and spent six hours in the cave. Then they went public, into business, charging forty centimes a visit; on the last Sunday of September there were three hundred visitors at two francs a head. The family who owned the land, the Rochefoucaulds, took over; the Abbé Breuil, that arbiter of authenticity, ratified the find. The artistic excellence of the Great Hall, its perfect preservation, became world renowned. Visitors streamed through. By the 1950s, the stream had enlarged to a lucrative torrent—more than a hundred thousand visitors each year. Bacteria from shoes and clothes accumulated on the paintings, and greenish algae lined the surface of the cave. Although they could control such growth with antibiotic sprays, the air itself— that inrush of modernity—threatened to undo in decades what millenia had preserved. The government closed Lascaux in 1963. Now, by application to the minister in Bordeaux, five visitors are permitted daily, five days a week; the waiting list is nearly two years long.

The fence is high. A guard dog patrols it. Two hundred meters down the hill, underground, they have re-created the original. Groups of up to forty people at a time pass through. We bought tickets for the final tour of Lascaux II that afternoon and waited in the heat. Our guide David was Welsh. He was thin and quick, a student of languages; he hoped to get his diploma next season from Aix-en-

Provence. We were his seventh group that day; a French group had preceded us, and Germans massed behind. He had a kind of priority, he told me, and would be rewarded with the real McCoy—the actual cave—at summer's end. He wore a T-shirt from the Hard Rock Cafe; his hair was springy, curling, and he told Andrea she should get a sweater from the car. A lady from California said, "First timers, right? I'm an old-timer, myself."

The outside door clanged shut. "You're in a decompression chamber," David said. It was darker and colder inside, and we let our eyes adjust. There were exhibits on the walls: an explanation of the tools that cave men used, a photograph of the four boys and their teacher and the dog. There were pictures of the original cave opening, when it was rocks and trees. Cro-Magnon man, said David, is not Neanderthal; put Cro-Magnon in a T-shirt, give him a shave and some after-shave lotion, and he's one of us. He winked at Cesca cozily: why you could meet Cro-Magnon at a dance.

Nowadays, David continued, we can reproduce the walls; we can replicate dimensions to the millimeter. A girl spent two years painting these; she used the same pigments and what we think were the original techniques. It's not as easy as it looks, he said; I know because I tried. Maybe it was two or three painters, maybe a kind of artisan class; what's amazing is how they built scaffolds and could do it on their backs.

So we advanced. He closed a second door and made

us wait. Watch your step, he told us, your eyes aren't used to this. The best way is to wait an hour, but that's closing time. I got a date this evening, and I can't be late. It's calcite, really, on the ceiling—carbonate of lime. *Homo sapiens sapiens* made their pigments with animal fat; then they let the fat evaporate out of hollow bones. Bones have been discovered lately, and vegetable tubes for blowing paint. They came in here with lamps. You couldn't see a thing otherwise, you have to imagine how dark it would be, how many lamps it took.

"It's cool," Francesca said.

"It isn't," said Andrea. "I don't need this sweater at all."

David flicked on the lights. The Great Hall jumped forward, its animals in flight. They had been familiar to me, in reproduction, for years. They were old friends. The black bull, the oxen, cows and horses, deer, the bison, and the ibex, their superimposed pregnant shapes, the canny way they crowded those who gaped at them in human herds and urged us on, converging, the brilliance of the color and delicate contour, the arrangement of rock—we made respectful noises; we gazed upwards and at each side.

David ran his flashlight down the flanks of the black bull. He pointed out a figure that they call the Unicorn. It has two horns, however, and a strange amalgam of human and animal shapes. Its sex is indeterminate, its attitude commanding, and it is one of a kind. So he said they believe it's a chief or shaman, some sort of witch doctor, maybe; see how these horses gather here, and how they run out of the hall.

It was a disappointment. It felt secondhand. I found myself thinking not of the four of us the first time in a cave, but of those boys in 1940 awe-struck by their find. Or perhaps they also took it for granted and thought it secondhand; there were many caves in the region, many stories of horses and bulls. Lascaux went commercial quickly and has remained that way.

The government's decision to impose controls, to simulate a cave with close caretaking accuracy, cannot but be praised. It is nonetheless the case that what we walked through had been opened to the public in July 1983, not closed by a rockfall eons before. The artist is known and alive. This is one paradox of democracy: the more widely available a site, the less special it becomes. Real-estate brokers, museum directors, advertising copywriters all profit from the strategy that this "once-in-a-lifetime opportunity" is yours and yours alone. What was authentic once—be it beach or wilderness, atelier or recipe—becomes its own derivative from the moment of discovery and praise. Call something inimitable, and it is mass-produced. Trumpet someone's love of privacy, and you increase their appeal. A test pilot celebrated for anonymity becomes a media celebrity twice over as a result. So Lascaux II felt like the television version of Lascaux, the postcard of a painting. And though David cheerfully reminded us not to forget the French injunction, "Don't forget the guide," I dropped my ten additional francs into his palm as reproof.

I was born in London, England, in 1942. My parents were German Jews who fled, separately, to England; there they were married in 1938. My elder brother, Thomas, was born two years to the day before Pearl Harbor. And family legend has it that when Hitler invaded Russia—thus diverting energy from an all-out assault on Great Britain—my mother turned to my father and said, "He's made a mistake. We may survive. Let's have another child."

So my small history begins with holocaust, and my first memories are of a city under siege. As a safety measure during the Blitz, our father transformed the garage. He made a sleeping shelter, painting circus animals on the inside walls. ARP, "air-raid precaution," became "a real pleasure" by virtue of design. An elephant leaned comfortably above my bed, its trunk curled down around the bedpost like a promise of support. A giraffe extended its long neck to where the ceiling met the wall and smiled down, silent, reassuring. Monkeys played catch with a lamp.

I thought of other caves—Tom Sawyer's cave in Hannibal, the caves of Elephanta, les grottes de Saint-Cézaire—the shapes one is asked to admire as adult or shrink from deliciously, young. At lunch in Ann Arbor one day, I told an expert on the Upper Paleolithic that I planned to visit Les Eyzies, and she said, "Yes, you should." France had seen the first and last great flowering of painting, I maintained, and maybe there was something in the dark within that ramified, that proved a source of light. This may be the distinction between animals glimpsed briefly on the

run and those domesticated animals in landscapes by Corot;
the distinction between hunter and farmer, kinesis and sta-
sis, the tribe that chases dinner or fattens it in fields. She
smiled; she let me ramble. It's the sort of small talk you
make under the influence of wine, or beauty, or a heavy
silence that urges you to speak.

It did seem strange, for instance, that human repre-
sentation should be so stilted in the caves, since the animals
are rendered with so sure a hand. The child who draws a
cow does so as clumsily or deftly as she draws herself. Yet
these cave humans are stick figures, not high art. The statuettes also are far less exact than those of the clay bison at
Tuc d'Audoubert. By comparison, the famous fertility figures look thick-fingered and amateurish; why should a pregnant woman be rendered less precisely than a pregnant
horse?

A recent theory that the statuettes were made by
pregnant women themselves—that such bulbous foreshort-
ening is faithful to a woman's-eye view of her own breasts
and belly—seems, though arguable, less than persuasive.
Was there some taboo on self-examination or simply an
absence of mirrors; did the painter take his band for granted
or fear for some reason to be too precise? At what point,
roughly speaking, did the sense of self—and most particularly the sense of self as artist—enter in?

The groupings in Lascaux and elsewhere seem a
sign; their significance, however, is an open question still.
They are by no means random, as Leroi-Gourhan has
shown; there is intention everywhere and veiled instruction
throughout. This is not "art for art's sake" or a cheerful
decoration of the more expensive caves; they represent

some version of the Chapel Perilous, a dark inward-turning to light.

Speleologists with the best modern equipment still find themselves endangered. Many have been injured, some have died. But to my knowledge there has been no ancient skeleton found lost in a cave's turning; either no one died within, or they traveled in groups and the bones were retrieved. How the children of the band were led to see the pictures; what they were shown when looking or returned outside to tell ("That was *fun,*" Francesca said. "That was weird," Andrea said. They bought postcards in quantity at the entrance booth.); how the artists were selected and how many of them worked at once; how rigorous the training and how widespread the skill: these are questions we may formulate but not decide. What we know is what we see.

The Hôtel de Centenaire at Les Eyzies-de-Tayac has a swimming pool. It boasts a first-rate restaurant and sumptuous guest apartments and waiters with white jackets and brightly polished shoes. Its stationery shows a pair of paleolithic deer.

In the course of the evening we acquired fliers for *Cap Blanc—Sculptures préhistoriques* and for the troglodyte citadel of La Roque-Saint-Christophe. These were affixed to the car. I had also been handed a brochure for *Le Thot— Musée Parc* and the *Grotte Gisement de Regourdou,* where we could park in the shade and admire the most ancient implement in the history of man! This antler fashioned into tool was visible in the museum, at the site of its discovery; a café-restaurant would offer us the panoramic vista each visitor deserves. By contrast, the Museum of Paleontology at Beyssac offered a permanent Diaporama on *"Les animaux de la préhistoire."* A *Tyrannosaurus rex* was just about to demolish a duck-billed *Trachodon;* there was also a display of cephalopods. A prehistoric scene showed Mousterian man, in the company of a child, engaged in brave single combat with a large bleeding bear. He wore a white loincloth; he hefted a spear. The bear was as good as impaled. There were javelins and many bones; there was a simulated fire in the cave.

In the bar beside the swimming pool they were playing Satchmo and Ray Charles. Elena and I ordered coffee and *poire.* A plane tree, glass-enclosed, was permitted to rise through the roof. A couple on their honeymoon from Boston said, "You *must* do Font de Gaume." We promised them we would; in the morning they were headed for the Pyrenees. "What's great about it," said the bride, "is that it's actual paintings there. An actual old-time cave."

We were in the traveler's suspended state—familiar with what went before, uncertain of what was to come. Soon enough, I told myself, our daughters will go separate ways, out of this protective orbit chancily. That others have done so before gave only the prospect of comfort. "Let's go inside," Elena said. "I'm tired. You have to be, too."

"Yes."

"The farms are working farms here, have you noticed?"

"Yes."

She stood. The waiter bobbed at us, his heels together, leaning.

The next day started wetly, with a thick valley mist. We stared through the window at striated rock. Color soaked down through the sky. Font de Gaume was open to the public as of nine o'clock. The children stayed in the hotel, and Elena and I drove to visit the cave. We joined the first group entering, this time with a French guide.

The entrance climb was steep, our number small. The guide had been there twenty years and was more compelled by it, she told us, every year. She had had the privilege, when they were lowering the floor to make a proper walkway, of finding a lamp here, and tools. She held them with these hands. She spread her hands.

She was fierce and dark and reverent; she spoke with precision and care, admiring the shapes' articulation, the authority of line. Font de Gaume had been discovered long before Lascaux. It was not difficult of access, and the weather had its way with the paintings over time. Alas, she said, the vandals—I cannot emphasize enough the disrespect, the degradation—painted on the paintings, making graffiti, etching their names. It is a desecration to those of us who feel we are inside a temple and that the artists were priests. You must ignore, so far as it is possible, the filth on this buffalo's shoulder, the shocking callow impulse to destroy. "I too exist," perhaps they were saying. "I also have a name." But I cannot forgive them, she said.

The passage was narrow and the vaulting high. We had to pay attention not to brush against the walls. By now I knew already a little of what to expect; it was therefore all the more superb, because unexpected, when she switched on the light. As the honeymoon couple from Boston had said, it was "an actual painting" at arm's length. I might have reached to touch it. Others had. There was a white grid of initials on the shank of a leaping immobilized bison; the frieze contained a dozen, once; and we could make out four. A fifth was a black smudge only, overlaid by calcite. We moved on.

Past the midpoint of the gallery, above eye level, dominant, are two long black curving antlers and the arched back of a stag. To the right, below, is a redness on the rock. Under the patient instruction of our guide we came to see the figures as a pair of deer, not locked in combat as elsewhere, but nuzzling and domestic: the black stag with its head bent down, the red head of a doe submissive at its feet. A version of this scene, in fact, had been emblazoned on the stationery of Le Centenaire. "It is the one example of tenderness, *tendresse,*" our guide maintained. "It is not a ferocity like those bison heading out into the valley, the cave-mouth."

There were tectiforms, or roof-shaped forms, four little horses, a mammoth, and a rhinoceros. Most of the animals were bison, with one ghostly human-seeming head having two black dots as eyes. The cave was cool. The guide praised the brilliance of conception, execution, the way a hollow in the rock could nonetheless suggest a shoulder's bulging muscle or a stomach big with child.

There is a dome-shaped niche towards the end. Inside that final private space small bison circled, dancing. The smallest fit inside a circular declivity; we crowded in to see. The others in our party murmured praise. Then they moved on. I stood at the rear of what felt like a chapel and knew myself, as not before, transfixed. This is where the journey starts; this is the linked chain. This is its own antidote and oxymoron: commencement, generation, those words that mean, equivalently, completion and beginning. *"Il faut sortir,"* she said. She said it gently. *"Il faut que nous nous en allions. On vous attend, Monsieur.* We must go. They are waiting. *N'oubliez pas le guide."*

II

❀

1961

Aubade: "A musical announcement of dawn, a sunrise song or open-air concert." This definition comes from the *Oxford English Dictionary*. The *Oxford Companion to English Literature* enlarges slightly on the term: "Aubade: (Provençal, *alba;* German, *Tagelied*) a dawn song, usually describing the regret of two lovers at their imminent separation. The form (which has no strict metrical pattern) flourished with the conventions of Courtly Love."

I first visited the south of France in 1961. I was eighteen years old and traveling for the first time without my family. The trip began in England, ended in Greece. I had just completed my sophomore year at Harvard College; I joined forces with a friend from MIT. We had checkpoints, of course, and some supervision—but it seemed the start of independence; we went to London, Amsterdam, Paris, Rome, Florence, Venice, Athens, and elsewhere. My friend was Greek; I flew home from the island of Rhodes. Home was suburban New York.

My father had provided me with a letter of credit from his bank, a system of funding long since replaced by traveler's checks or credit cards. It was outdated even then, but it fairly reeked of tradition—of young sons from old

23

families being ushered into counting rooms, of doors easing shut behind them with a firm managerial click. I was grateful for the funding and glad of the cachet. Also, I needed the admonitory limit of the letter ("Please be advised that his credit does not exceed . . ."). My first night abroad I was robbed. We were staying in a bed-and-breakfast near Marble Arch; I was punch-drunk on travel and drunk on my second pub-scotch. Next day I found my wallet on the bathroom floor, the pound notes in it gone.

"There's nothing left." I turned the wallet inside out. There were documents, no cash.

"Jesus," said my friend. His name was Paul. "What happened?"

"I must have dropped it on the floor."

"Welcome to England," he said. He liked to say that he, a Greek, feared the English bearing gifts.

"They took it all."

"Your passport too?"

I pointed. "No."

"Jesus. What a country."

The letter of credit remained. That afternoon—shaved, sober—I presented myself at the bank. Had I traveled with money in hand, I would have squandered it soon.

What we squander is retained in that memory palace, the past. My own begins a few miles north of Marble Arch, in a London under siege. Tolstoy claimed to remember the womb. I cannot distinguish, however, which memories are actual and what I recollect being told till I nodded in acknowledgement and said, yes, yes, that's right. In order of ascending probability, these things: the blackout and air raid the day I was born, the neighbor who brought jam to the house because my mother shouted so in childbirth, the air-raid shelter with its comforting menagerie in bright paint on the rock.

My mother's brother arrived from America, bearing coffee and bananas. I remember loving chocolate in its rationed scarcity; we kept chickens, and once they escaped. We lived in Hampstead Garden Suburb, a short walk from the Heath. I remember hedgehogs in the road, a stand of trees at the crest of our hill that I called Sherwood Forest. We had gooseberry bushes, and gooseberry jam. I learned how to whistle before my brother could, and therefore tormented him, whistling. There was fog so whitely thick at night that our father walked in front of the car, using the beams as a lantern. The house he searched for and we found was brick, with a circular driveway: Number 23, Holne Chase.

I was known as Nick the Looker, close to the ground and downward-focused; even today I spot four-leaf clovers more readily than I can recognize birds. Once, our mother lost a jewel from a ring in the pebbles of the driveway, and we spent hours sifting through the pebbles; she had promised a reward. I had no doubt I'd find the stone and earn the promised pound. My brother did. He saw the head of Minerva in a section I'd not yet scoured, and I was so outraged by the inequity that I set up a howl. Our mother came running. "I found it," he said. The ring had value; I too had looked. I got ten shillings as a consolation prize. We were spoiled, of course, and doted on, but this was my first lesson in the way of the world's rewards: cry persuasively enough and a beneficent committee may give you second prize.

My mother's family were bankers in Berlin, my father's in the import-export business in Hamburg. As their name suggests, the Delbancos had been Italian bankers, money-lenders in Venice originally. One of them, Anselmo Delbanco, had been sufficiently munificent in the fifteenth century to stand as a plausible model for Shylock: a merchant who floated the fleet. In 1630 the Delbancos went to Germany, remaining there for three hundred years. And often, in my childhood, I had the sense of diminution: of pictures in museums that had once been in the family, of chauffeurs and upstairs maids and cooks who fled at Hitler's advent, leaving the cupboard bone-bare.

It's a heightened fantasy. We were never all that rich and never poor. The furniture was hefty, plush, the china and silver intact. A certain smell of polish—a thickness of cigarette smoke in the air, the floors and sideboards thickly waxed, nuts and Sacher torte waiting uncovered—hovers in my nostrils still. In my memory, the light is strong; my mother disliked candles. The walls are dark with objects, which the maid must dust at peril: African masks, shields and totems of all sorts, pre-Columbian statuary, graphic work of Goya, Rembrandt, and, particularly, Lautrec. We called a funerary figure from China "The Chinese Lady"; a demon-mask hung in the entrance hall. I used to take comfort in the certainty no robber would be brave enough to pass beneath those protuberant eyes and that bristling horsehair beard. There were ceremonial jade blades. I practiced hefting chieftains' spears, glared balefully back at monkey skulls and masks covered with antelope skin. My father had—has—an "eye." Jane Avril would lift her multicolored leg above my bed, and Yvette Guilbert stared soulfully down. Goya's toreador gestured imperiously at a dying bull an arm's length away on the stairwell; Aristide Bruant turned his black back upon conversation in the library. Portraits of my mother as a girl or her mother in a garden stood cater-corner to a battle-god, his wooden bulk studded with nails.

 I'm told I was a placid child, and plump. My father's mother called me Buddha because I sat cross-legged and smiling in the pram; when we first went to the seashore, I said, "My, what a big puddle." I attended Miss Jamaica's kindergarten down the road; my brother went to the King Alfred School. I remember sitting on the coal pile by the chute or playing king of the castle with Robert Elkeles—he was the dirty rascal, and we pelted each other with coal. We had a red-headed cook called Kathleen who had glass in her thumb; it acted up something terrible, she told me, once a month. There was the excitement of tunnels in the tube and an advertisement for Coleman's Mustard ("You must not eat the nation's meat without the nation's mustard"). I could *read*. We visited the Isle of Wight, Trafalgar Square, a green frog-fountain in Wengen where the frog emitted water from its mouth. Often, we visited France. Those·of my mother's family who did escape the Nazis had done so by fleeing to Paris, then, slowly, south and west. France, she used to tell us, was a civilized nation, a place to retreat to: heart's home.

So when the time came for the trip, I asked my parents what to see. We were sitting in the library, the atlas spread between us, all Europe on a page. My father made a vague, inclusive gesture at the crease; my mother was more definite. "Paris," she said. "Then go south. You must end where it's already half-Italian: Nice."

Yet this particular journey starts with a girl named Dianne. I had met her in 1960, at the end of the previous spring. Dianne wanted to be a performer; she sang, danced, and played the piano. She studied the guitar. She was long-legged, tall, and long-haired in the fashion of the time. She had the remnants of a stammer and a forthright anxiety; she would tell you she was nervous, fearful, shy. She said that her family left her feeling insecure, unloved, and that her comic antics were a ploy to gain attention. She had a "worry-bump" she rubbed until the skin grew red and chafed, the way a violinist's neck-flesh grows abraded. Most of all, she told me, she was frightened of being ignored. She had clamored for applause throughout her childhood, to make her father smile at her, to make her mother proud.

"But you're wonderful," I said.

"No."

"Your sisters aren't that wonderful."

"They are. One of them is glamorous and one of them an angel. They lick the platter clean."

"There's room for you."

"There isn't. No."

On stage, however, she lost all such uncertainty; she

gathered the light of the room. Her presence grew definite, charged. This was true before there was a stage—when sitting at a piano or singing from the makeshift platform of a porch. Dianne had a deep, strong, throaty voice, an erotic abandon. I thought her a star from the start.

She lived in Riverdale, New York, and was attending Sarah Lawrence College. Her house was large, with bedrooms in the attic we could lock. Her father had been ill for years; he died shortly after we met. Mr. Levy's diminished presence and the hushed sense of the sickroom had done much to make her adolescence the unhappy thing she thought it. His withdrawal felt, she told me, like reproach.

Her father rarely spoke. He sat stony-faced in an armchair all day, wearing pajamas and a bathrobe, hands folded in his lap. He was wealthy, had been powerful; signed photographs of famous men (Jackie Robinson, Dwight David Eisenhower, Albert Einstein) lined the stairwell and the halls. Corporations bore his name. His wife maintained something like a salon; there were always visitors—musicians, politicians, refugees and actors, authors—in the downstairs library or spilling out onto the lawn.

On one such occasion I met a woman named Eloise. She was perhaps forty years old, very French, and a television personality in Paris. She had the brittle chic that renders failure graceful, and she had not failed. Her husband, however, had died. In retrospect I think perhaps he'd left her for a new companion, or elected solitude—but I am not sure. She came to visit Dianne's mother as if in shared bereavement. I served drinks. I did so, often, at those soirées; I was the new man of the house.

There was a concert grand piano in the living room,

with chairs and couches facing it. At some point in the evening, always, someone asked for music and the Levys would oblige. There were three daughters—Dianne the youngest—and a son. They offered show tunes, operetta, opera, folk songs, torch songs, the blues. The three girls took turns performing or joined in duets and trios; their brother photographed them all. Then a guest would play Chopin or Liszt, and Dianne would return to my side. She was wonderful, I told her, perfect, better than ever, the best. Play "John Henry" again, I would ask her, or "Danny Boy" or "Down in the Valley" or "Ol' Devil Moon"; sing again.

Eloise said I should call her in Paris; I agreed. She said she would welcome my visit; she had known the Levys forever, I must most certainly call.

In Paris it developed that I could do her a favor. She had a busy schedule and a lover named Claude. He had a villa in Juan-les-Pins, and they wanted her car in the south, but they would rather take the *wagon-lit* and have me deliver it; would I very much mind? I could see the countryside, and they would be unwearied by the drive.

Her car was a Simca Aronde. It was a white convertible with two red seats and a transmission that I could not use. I had barely earned my driver's license, had never driven a stick shift before. But Paul—my traveling companion—was confident with sports cars, certain he could teach me how to drive. We told her, therefore, yes. We took down her address in Juan-les-Pins; we borrowed Claude's *Guide Michelin,* assured them we would see them soon, and headed south. I pretended to a recently sprained ankle as we left and hobbled to the passenger seat. Paul drove. Dianne, too, had been in Paris, traveling with an aunt and uncle, and she stood waving by the curb. Fare forward, voyager, we'll meet again in Rome.

"The Journey, Not the Arrival, Matters." So wrote Leonard Woolf. And it was a fine, full journey: the first sight of Chartres, the increasing ease with second gear, the castles of the Loire, a festival in Orléans, a rainstorm in Clermont-Ferrand. What matters here, however, is arrival. We came, on the third day, to the hill village of Les Baux-de-Provence. I had done some reading on its bloody history, its troubadours and prideful lords of Baux—"warriors all, vassals never," claims Mistral.

Yet what we looked for then was food, and the celebrated restaurant beneath the village walls. L'Oustau de Baumanière was and, to a degree, still is a remarkable place to eat; the food is Provençal in emphasis, the decor selfconsciously simple, the prices (we had scrimped the night before) just barely in range.

Our little car was dusty. Its convertible top was down. I had learned to use the gearshift and was sure of my ability to negotiate the parking lot—at ease with our windswept informality, the clattering racket of travel. The other cars were Jaguars, Lancias, Maseratis; they gleamed. Where we had taken pride of place we now looked pinched and poor. An attendant appeared, disapproved. By the time I had shut off the engine, he produced a hose. We closed the top; he sprayed it. As we walked into the restaurant, he was adding soap.

The maître d'hôtel received us in much the same way. He raised his eyebrows, narrowed his eyes; he took our names and promised a table with condescending aplomb. We were ushered to an anteroom, given menus, given time. When I made a selection, he begged to disagree. There were tomatoes in the first course I had ordered; surely I did not intend to have tomatoes also in the sauce for the fish dish? When he had corrected us, commended our discerning choice, and identified the wines we would most certainly want to select, he said, "An hour, gentlemen? We will call you; you might wish to swim."

There was a pool. We swam. Men with tight black bathing suits and women not plausibly their wives were lounging by the pool. Sipping apéritifs, the two of us lay back and dreamed of earned access to such elegance; twenty minutes before our table was ready we were invited to dress.

What followed was delight. I have eaten at Baumanière several times since and at restaurants around the world with arguably better chefs at inarguably less cost. But few meals I remember have provided such excitement: we were travelers made welcome, for a price. The staff hovered and offered and poured. They clucked approvingly at our expressed approval; they pointed with justifiable pride to the cheese and wheeled in the laden sweet-cart.

We lurched and rumbled off to Nîmes, through Saint-Rémy and Arles. The rest of the day is a jumble: amphitheaters, olive groves, Daudet's *Moulin,* bright reaches in the fading light that looked as if composed expressly by van Gogh. It is an emptied cornucopia: Toulon, the aftertaste of wine metallic in my mouth, Hyères and Presqu'ile de Giens, and finally a hotel by the water, which we could hear, not see.

The southern coast of France is roughly three hundred fifty miles long; its perpendicular bisector, roughly, is the Rhône. In one sense the whole region can be called Provence, since all of it was once Provincia Romana. Yet Nice belonged to Piedmont for five hundred years, and the towns beneath the Pyrenees still feel like Catalonia; *le vrai Provence* is less than the Midi.

Archibald Lyall, writing his companion guide to *The South of France* in 1963, has this to say:

> With the inland region of upper Provence . . . this book is not concerned. It is poor and mountainous, and the population of its little towns and its hill-top villages, unable to live on scenery alone, is steadily dwindling, drained away to the rich and bustling towns of . . . the Coast.

But Gordes and Roussillon of the Vaucluse are as fashionable now as were Saint-Paul-de-Vence and Eze-Village then, or Hyères and Sanary before. The living made "on scenery alone" has grown very good indeed. Laurence Wylie, who wrote of Roussillon in *Village in the Vaucluse* and is in part responsible for its celebrity, reports that he was offered a windmill and the hill on which it stood for ninety dollars in 1950. In the summer of 1959, to his astonishment, "The Notaire told me that vacant lots which could not be sold ten years ago for $150 are now worth $2,000 an acre." And in the decades since, there has been exponential increase.

Ford Madox Ford—whose ghost will haunt these pages, and whose *Provence* is crucial to them—puts the problem precisely:

> Or, once more, there are the parasitic bathing towns of the Côte d'Azur, the French Riviera, which both historically and geographically are in Provence. . . . They have arisen where the Alps begin to crowd in on the Mediterranean and they have arisen there because the light foam of that sea frets their expanses of sand whilst the mountains shelter them from the mistral. To say that these little cities of rather mechanical and monotonous pleasure are not true Provence would be as unjust to them as it would be to Provence to include them.

His Fordian and magisterial definition of the area takes Lyons as the apex of a triangle, an inverted capital V that has the Mediterranean as its base. This too is bisected by the Rhône. The right-hand side, stretching down to the Alps, is "true Provence," the left mere Gallia Narbonensis. It is a vexed question. Ask a company of devotees if the Bouches-du-Rhône lie in Provence, and the answer is certainly yes; ask them if the Var belongs, and there will be demurrals; ask of the Alpes-Maritimes, and the answer is certainly not.

It is a country of the mind, a way of saying "yes" that renders assent emphatic—langue d'oc rather than langue d'oïl—a preference for olive oil and garlic in cuisine. The true Provençal, they will tell you, is laughter-loving yet aloof; he will welcome strangers but keep an inward distance; he has been conquered often but never quite subdued. There is a strain of gypsy and a hint of *montagnard,* a pagan pleasure in the light and ritual propitiation of the dark river god; the troubadours were here, and Templars, and Albigensians, and Adamites, and the Babylonian captivity took place in Avignon.

Next morning we set off along the coast. Paul planned to be an architect; he lectured me about the influence of Roman road- and bridge-building techniques. He knew about Le Corbusier's work in Marseilles, about the flying buttress and the sacred grove. He wanted to combine skyscrapers and the Romanesque.

Paul had charm, some recklessness, and a good deal of sexual bravado. Our ways would part. He became a nightclub owner and New York restaurateur; he dabbled in Hollywood also. He concerned himself, I heard, with the decor of his ventures—places where you paid, for instance, to break plates. The last I heard he was operating a barbecued chicken franchise in Forest Hills.

My own pretensions were literary. Ernest Hemingway had killed himself in Ketchum, Idaho, that summer. It was the start of July. When the news reached Paris I took it as a private grief and personal injunction; I planned to drink to Papa's memory in every bar he wrote about on the Left Bank. These were legion. By the time I toasted him at Le Select, Aux Deux Magots, at the Brasserie Lipp and Café Flore, I understood my number too was legion. Earnest young men in his image were everywhere, raising their glasses or wheeling through the Luxembourg Gardens, saying "Isn't it pretty to think so," hunting their Hadley or Brett.

I was also reading *The Alexandria Quartet*. Justine, Melissa, Clea, and their lush companions danced down the page alluringly; though I wanted to drink like a Hemingway hero, I was word-drunk on Durrell. That final day in Paris, I woke up spitting blood. This seemed to me appropriate: the badge of Keats, of Chatterton and Crane. (The night before, a woman in a bar had looked at me and said, *"Tiens, les yeux d'un poète."* She must have been surprised at my acquiescent reticence; the line would have been profitable with other boys before. But I took it as my due. I *did* have the eyes of a poet; I had my darling muse Dianne and the notion of fidelity, and we would meet again soon.)

So the blood seemed a red badge, a mark of vocation. I coughed. It turned out that I had burst a capillary on my tonsil; by the time I saw a doctor there was nothing left to see. Paul paid me no attention; he disliked the sight of blood. Our hero therefore dreams of Alexandria or Montmartre in the twenties, of ambassadors and warriors who make him welcome, bowing, of renown for his as-yet unwritten epic of the self, of pink-stained handkerchiefs and roses strewn by virginal barmaids who bend to his bed, of valorous deeds and recitals—the daring young man in a Simca Aronde. This afternoon he plays a character out of Fitzgerald ("It's about half past one." "It's not a bad time," said Dick Diver. "It's not one of the worst times of the day"). He fetches up in Juan-les-Pins and follows the directions for Les Pins Parasols.

Eloise and Claude had changed. They were less gracious, less delighted to see us. They did not invite us in. I handed her the keys. The car had grown dusty again; the flowers we proffered were wilting. Perhaps she thought we hoped to stay the night or for a meal; perhaps we arrived on the wrong day. She pointed to a bus stop and the public road for Cannes.

Most probably, I think now, she and Claude were arguing or about to make plans or make love. Most likely our arrival had interrupted something that had its own imperative and would continue when we left. The car had been delivered; that was that. Claude waited on the balcony of Les Pins Parasols, smoking, tapping his foot. She said, "Give my best to the Levy *ménage,*" and turned, skirt swirling, away. We gathered our bags from the trunk of the car and walked to the bus stop to wait.

As with the meal at Les Baux, there were ritual observances I could not then observe. In *Tender Is the Night,* when Rosemary watches Dick Diver, she does so with a sense of charmed exclusion—and sets herself to be included by the charming circle on the *plage.* I never did see Eloise again in person, though I later watched her with regularity on French television. There had been some test we did not know we had failed, some way of adult worldliness in which we proved deficient. "The bitch," Paul said. "The bitch. She treats us like chauffeurs."

That night in Cannes we played roulette. It seemed the thing to do. We had been planning it, preparing, working out a system now for weeks. Paul had had training in statistics, and I too liked arithmetic; we both played poker in Cambridge and fancied ourselves old hands. Our plan was a "sure thing."

It was a variation on doubling—odds or evens, red or black. We would cover ourselves for the zeros and gamble one-tenth of our winnings on quadrants, one-twentieth each on a hunch. We also would tip the croupier. One of us would place the bet, the other would give orders from a chart. We worked this out in detail, wore our most grownup attire—we were not yet twenty-one and therefore had to bluff our way past the indifferent guards—and sauntered in.

The casino was impressive. With its shabby grandeur, its windows giving out onto the bay (an American battleship riding at anchor, white lights garlanding the silhouette, yachts clustered like so many goslings near its hull; later there would be an "incident," a mistaken release of engine oil, and the Riviera beaches would be soiled, and sailors worked for days with rakes and rags to clean the *plage,* and the Sixth Fleet moved its prideful presence back and cut the lights), I could almost imagine the casino peo-

pled with prose, as if Dick Diver drank with Count Mip-
pipopolous, and Capodistria ogled the whores, as if Jake
Barnes or Darley might be smoking, supervisory: those
literary gentlefolk who witnessed the rich at their sport. We
bought our chips; we sat. A white-haired woman sneezed.
We watched the table for a while and pulled out our chart.
    *"Messieurs, 'dames, faites vos jeux. Les jeux sont faits.
Rien ne va plus."* We played two nights. We won. It was not
much money, but it paid for our stay in the south. It was
beginner's luck. We followed our game plan scrupulously,
losing only on our hunches, tipping the croupier each time
he shoveled chips our way, providing a kind of diversion
perhaps for others near the wheel. They smiled and nodded
at us, two studious children doubling on black. They lifted
drinks; they smoked.
    I know now our system was false. The laws of proba-
bility had nothing to do with our winning; odds on the
roulette wheel favor the house. And I have never won
again—in that casino, or in any other—at roulette. *"Les jeux
sont faits."* We won, I think, because the croupiers decided
we should, or did not mind, or sensed that if they reeled us
in we might prove lifelong fish. If there be such a thing as
instinct—the premonitory certainty of rightness in a bet—
then instinct served us well those nights. We won because
we did not know we ought to lose.

Certain vistas move us; others fade. Some are compelled by
mountains, while some visit valleys instead. For each pil-

grim to the desert there is one who dreams of forests; for each lover of the lakefront there is one who wants the river; some are happiest on oceans, some near ponds. There's little point in ranking landscape, in claiming for the Himalayas beauty greater than the Hindu Kush, or asserting that the Yucatán's more vivid than Bermuda. The point is to identify one's own true north, the compass grid that signifies one's bodily coordinates: *this* matters, *that* does not.

I was born in England, of parents born in Germany, with an Italian name. I live and work in Michigan and also in Vermont. The notion of elected roots has personal consequence, clearly. This is the rule, not the exception, in our mobile time. Most of us live elsewhere than our parents' parents; many of us improvise an answer to the question, "Where do you come from, where's home?" And the traveler who's seen the Himalayas and the Hindu Kush, who has been to Merida as well as Tucker's Town, may be forgiven if his answers sound improvised at times. At any rate, I hope so, since from time to time I've answered "Home? The south of France."

Those periods now seem emblematic; they represent stages of age. I visited the south of France alone and with my parents; I settled there to write my first book and, later, with my wife. We lived there with our elder daughter when she was young, and now again as she tilts towards adolescence. This summer, with two children, I am as much the proper citizen as was my father when he furnished me with credit at the bank. Since the wheel continues circling, I want to follow its track. One aspect of the autobiographical impulse, possibly, has to do with circumscription—with just such provisional tracking down the arc of a limned life. We have *been* here; this is our image; this is what we saw. In the lower right-hand corner note the maker's mark. The sense of self as witness antedates Lascaux.

From Cannes Paul and I took the train to Nice, from Nice to Rome. My sojourn in the south of France had lasted less than a week. The world was full of wonders then, and this rapid transit left me dreaming of return. The reader will have noticed, as Ford Madox Ford was fond of saying, that the question of credit remains. The letter of credit sufficed. I took a steamer out of Venice where my family first took its name, saw the Parthenon and lazed along the harbor in Rhodes. I encountered my first corpse and turned nineteen.

III

✳

1987

In my green and student days, *Village in the Vaucluse* was hailed as a seminal text. The *New York Times* called it "sociology rich in human overtones," the *New Yorker* praised its "grace and humor," and Henri Peyre himself, in the *Saturday Review,* said, "Seldom, if ever, has the daily life of a humble French community been delineated with such patience, such smiling tolerance, such objectivity." We studied this account of life in a French village; we listened to its author, Laurence Wylie, lecture. We were grateful for the great good luck of having him in class.

He was soft-spoken, affable, definite; he had a shock of reddish hair then starting to go white. He wore chinos and tweed coats and what I think were horn-rimmed glasses—the very definition of a Cambridge intellectual. Yet he seemed self-effacing. I was not. My undergraduate thesis had the jaw-breaking title of "A Comparison of *Les Trophées* by José Maria de Heredia and the *Neue Gedichte* of Rainer Maria Rilke, with Close Analysis of "La Naissance d'Aphrodité" and "Geburt der Venus." In order to be graduated from that honors program, I needed to defend my thesis and pass an oral examination. There was a committee of three.

The committee chairman, a fearsome scholar, grilled me at length. The others (my thesis advisor and the great Wylie himself) kept silent. At the end of the session, the chairman asked, "Mr. Delbanco, in *The Charterhouse of Parma,* Stendhal's hero engages in the Battle of Waterloo. From what vantage does he fight?"

This was a book I had read. I answered, with relief, "From the mud, sir. He watches Waterloo entirely covered by mud." Laurence Wylie approved. He said, "No further questions," and they conferred my degree.

I had seen Wylie once or twice, read of him once or twice in years to come. But he surely did not know me, and I doubt I would have known him had we stood in the same shopping line. It came to pass, however, through one of those skeins of linkage (the mother of our neighbor in Ann Arbor has a friend . . .) that the house we have rented in Lourmarin is where—when in the south of France—Laurence Wylie lives.

I had told my friend and neighbor that we planned to go—though we did not know precisely where—to France. The house near Grasse we used to live in, I explained, was sold. He said he knew a place we could maybe settle, did not know its name, knew only that Albert Camus was buried in the village. Next day he told us "Lourmarin, and you can rent the house." I had never heard of Lourmarin before. The atlas did not help. We dug out our old *Michelin* and located the Lubéron range—an inch above the Mediterranean, a half-inch from Aix-en-Provence. Avignon was to the west, Marseilles the south. A knowledgeable traveler said, "Lourmarin. Yes, I've been there. They make a brilliant white wine." And once I learned that Laurence

Wylie was the man whose house we'd occupy, all doubt was replaced by desire; what was good enough for him was surely so for us. We arranged the rental and, while still in America, received directions and the front-door key.

From Les Eyzies to Lourmarin is a long day's driving, though it seems short on the map. We arrive at dusk. The road out of Avignon has heavy afternoon traffic; the main streets of Cavaillon and Lauris do not beguile the passerby; the fruit sold in the roadside stands looks pinched and poor. We drive through flatlands slowly rising; the heat does not abate. There are fields of sunflowers, then lavender, then vineyards on the slope.

The landscape feels familiar, not because we have been here but have seen it painted: the geometric outcroppings of rock, the plane trees and the cypress-spires and the high white wisps of cloud above the foothills north. The sign for Lourmarin is painted on a wooden arrow where we veer, sharply, left. A fat man on a bicycle looks up at us, disdainful of the squealing wheels; Elena says he should have breadsticks jutting from a basket on his back.

Our rented house sits on a hill near the village; the directions are precise. We find Sauge et Thyme with no trouble; wild thyme sprouts through the driveway gravel and sage in the red clay. The view—that part of it that has not been blocked off by trees—is expansive: the Château de Lourmarin, a town hall, churches, shops and fields, and then the Lubéron range.

This house is large, a twenty-year-old version of the ancient style, built of stucco over cinder block, not stone. The roof is tiled. The flooring too is tile, the walls white plaster. We unpack and settle in, opening the shutters, then the windows, turning on the lights. There is a television set, a spanking-clean set of appliances, even a garbage disposal. How many houses have I entered as a stranger and made of them at least a temporary shelter? The *gardien* passes by to verify that we do indeed belong. We brandish our key. His breath is rank with whiskey; he invites me for a drink. I indicate our suitcases, our daughters, our jumbled supplies. "Come tomorrow instead, then," he says.

Elena likes the rooms, the view. There is a white slice of moon. She rearranges furniture and makes the children's beds, turning on the radio so there will be music while we work.

One notion I had had (increasingly unlikely in the increasing present) was to find a Frenchman who had traveled to the New World from this region years before. The French had been the first white men to travel through Michigan, the state we now call home; the voyages of Père Marquette, La Salle, Champlain, and others had organized my nightly reading for a year. The French who crisscrossed Michigan, it stood to reason, had gone there out of duty or devotion or ambition or disgrace. They spawned lilac bushes and place-names and children and moved on north, west, and south; I hoped to find some lesser Cadillac from some little town in Provence.

This did not work. The explorers were Normans or Bretons or Gascons. A few had sailed out of Marseilles. But I could find no Provençal explorer, no meridional man of note who settled in our part of the New World. And the more I thought about it, the less vivid the idea. Frenchman goes to Michigan in 1687; three hundred years thereafter, the novelist returns.

This restlessness, this rootlessness—how many times have I impersonated competence or counterfeited certainty? It's a familiar feeling, the sense of self adrift. Yet I doubt my brothers have it, doubt even my father has it who lives in the third country of which he is a citizen. And there's nothing to complain of, no actual cause for self-pity, as I settle to the couch. The rooms are clean, well lit. There are bottles and cans on the shelves. Outside, the dark deepens; the first stars appear.

At five o'clock next morning, we drive down to Aix-en-Provence. Linda Miller, a student and friend from Ann Arbor, is due to arrive there at six. She will spend a month in Lourmarin, helping with the household, trading time with our daughters—who adore her—for a roof. We meet the train, but Linda is not on it. This is unlike her, disconcerting; at least she could have called. There is only one station in Aix. The next train from Paris, or one with a connection at Marseilles, arrives in two hours; we wait. The croissants in the railroad café are expensive and stale, the coffee too bitter. The children grow alarmed: Linda does not speak much French, we have no way of reaching her, she has no way—without us—to get to our village and house.

The eight o'clock train barely pauses. A dozen passengers, none of them Linda, get off. This is pointless, I announce, we can't wait all morning, we ought to go back and she'll call. In Lourmarin it develops, however, that the telephone *est coupée.* The line has been cut off. This explains her silence. I fiddle with the entry box fruitlessly, checking connections, changing the fuses and plug. It is Sunday morning. The *gardien* totters by, wearing what he wore last night, to remind me of that promised drink, and when I explain our problem he says it isn't serious, not grave, he'll keep an eye out for the American blonde and we can use his machine. I don't need to make a call, I tell him, I'm waiting for one, and the phone doesn't work. *Dommage,* he says, that's serious, but in this village we'll find her, nobody gets lost.

Astonishingly, he is right. At five o'clock that afternoon two cars appear—the *gardien* triumphant, blatting his horn, then Linda in the passenger seat of a car piloted by a waiter from a restaurant in Aix. She reached the station at noon, having missed her connection in Marseilles, and the young damsel in distress aroused what we might as well call the waiter's chivalric instincts, and he offered her a lift. They found Lourmarin, then our hill, then our house. He stammers with pleasure, claps his broad hands. He is, however, late for work and has to turn around. I attempt to pay him, but the payment that he hopes for is a date. "Linda," he says, "that means pretty." She promises to call. We will not connect the telephone, however; it is not a promise she feels obliged to keep.

Les Magnanarelles, where we are staying, consists of two dozen houses on this collective hill. In America it might be called a subdivision, but the word seems inaccurate here; the building lots have taken twenty years to sell. Some houses therefore appear long-entrenched; others are under construction. A map at the guarded entrance to the hill proclaims *Terrain à Vendre;* two lots remain. The road makes a long, steep circle. There is no exit from the top.

The owners are Parisian, mostly, or from Geneva or Lyons. Their houses are expensive, with pools and land-scaped grounds. Those who have retired live here year-round; the majority appear to use it as a weekend retreat. Les Magnanarelles is an invented word, not easy to translate; it means, most nearly, "the place where silkworms live." *Une magnanerie* is a silkworm nursery, and the mulberry trees crucial to silkworms were fecund here once, apparently. Now the plantings on the slope are various and tended, and what trees flourish by themselves are pine.

The caretaker's house squats at the viewless bottom of our hill. The entrance drive is private, with a gate. The gate doors, however, are large and vine-encumbered; they do not seem to close. Jacques the *gardien* was a soldier till he shot himself in the foot. He wears a Cardin T-shirt and pink pants. His eyes are small, red-rimmed; he rubs them often, coughing. I have yet to see him sober. There are paper bags and bottles by the mailbox of each house he watches while the owners are away. His military bearing is a point of pride, however; he tells me that he fought at Dien Bien Phu. "You Americans," he shakes his head. "We could have told you it was hopeless. I could have told you that in 1954."

He has a special fondness for the general across the road—an old, bent man I wave to who does not wave back. This neighbor's hair is white; he uses a walker; he seems deaf. He takes his constitutional at eight o'clock each morning, promptly, and then again at three. Jacques the *gardien* tells me, *"Nous nous comprenons.* We understand each other, the general and I. We are military men, we speak of old campaigns."

The notion of these two in spirited rehearsal of shared battles seems improbable. As if he suspects my suspicion, Jacques insists. *"Si, si,"* he says. *"Mon géneral.* We get along together very well."

The history of southern France is various and brutal—not more so than in other sections of the Mediterranean, perhaps, but various enough. Old campaigners feel at home. The Midi has been subject to invasion, claims, and counterclaims since soldiering began. Those who built the first stone ramparts by the sea and those who assaulted them have fought since Tyrrhenia sank—leaving Corsica, the Esterel and the Balearics behind. Some of the earliest traces of man are found in the hills above Nice.

But recorded local wrangling starts, by most accounts, with Phocaeans from Asia Minor and the founding of Massalia, now Marseilles. The Carthaginians unsettled those first Greeks in 542 B.C. and remained in residence for sixty years. On his overland journey from Spain in 218 B.C., Hannibal passed through Provence. His elephants, no doubt, would have found it easy going—by comparison, at least, with what was to come. He must have wondered, in the Alps, if Italy was worth the visit or the climb. There were lemon trees behind him and ice-covered passes ahead.

The Romans founded Aix-en-Provence a century thereafter. The Celts were threatening, and Marseilles requested help. In 102 B.C., Marius defeated the Teutons near Aix; then, from 58 to 51 B.C., Julius Caesar conquered "all Gaul." Direct rule was imposed under Augustus, and Roman civilization flourished in the area for several hundred years. Nîmes, Arles, Vaison-la-Romaine, and the roads and bridges everywhere attest to Roman rule. In 476 A.D., it collapsed.

Then came Vandals, Alemanni, Visigoths, Ostrogoths, Franks; Hungarians sailed up the Rhône; Normans landed in the Camargue. In the ninth century alone, there were four separate Moorish invasions. The hill villages—quixotic in the present context—make considerable sense when looked at in this light. Armies would advance on them like killer ants; it helped to have some warning, some time to boil the oil.

The first of the great plagues leveled Provence in 1348. The local notary, whose records commence in the fifteenth century, wondered aloud what had happened before; when reminded that there had been no one alive in Lourmarin to register, he slapped his forehead, blushing, and said, *"Tiens, que je suis bête.* How stupid. I simply forgot."

The country is wind-swept continually. As with those northern peoples who have various terms describing ice, there are many words here for the nature of the wind. These are the thirty-two winds of Provence: Tramountano, Tems-Dré, Mountagnero, Ventouresco, Aguieloun, Cisampo, Gregau, Auro-Bruno, Levant, Auro-Rousso, Vent-Blanc, Marin-Blanc, Eissero, Auro-Caudo, Vent de Souleu, En Bas, Marin Mie Jour, Vent de Bas, Foui, Vent Larg, Labé, Vent di Damo, Poumentau, Rousau, Narbounès, Travesso, Manjo Fango, Cers, Mistrau, Vent d'Aut, Biso, and Auro-Drecho.

It has been blowing all night. The dead pine needles on the porch have eddied and collected as if swept. They make a pile behind the wall like a brown sleeping dog.

Andrea likes to draw. Each morning we gather flowers, arrange them in a vase, and scrupulously she copies what she sees. I work outside, on the tile patio, and she joins me there in the second wicker chair. She has a drawing pad and watercolors and Caran d'Ache crayons and pencils in ranked rows; she places the vase on the table and outlines it lightly in pencil, then fills in the shape.

"Why don't you draw the step?" I say. "Those steps there, by the table."

She shakes her head.

"Why don't you make it blue?"

"It isn't."

"It *could* be."

"Not this step, Daddy. It's orange."

"If you made it blue it would look that way to anyone who saw the picture."

"They'd be wrong," she says.

"Don't be so certain, darling. How do you know what that painter was seeing—the one we looked at yesterday—when he painted castles. Maybe he was dreaming them."

"He wasn't."

"Maybe he dreamed them so clearly that all these years later we see what he saw the day he shut his eyes."

"This step is orange," she says.

We settle into Sauge et Thyme, Professor Wylie's place. He has remarried lately, and his wife owns this house. I am surrounded by his documents, his photographs and maps of walks to take, his books. He must be nearly eighty now, long since emeritus. Larry (or so his friends call him) is a kind of patron saint of the region, at least to those who read. His description of "Peyrane" has had much to do with the renascence of Roussillon, Peyrane's original. His coats hang in the closets here, his shirts and pants are shelved.

There is a list of things to do for guests: a short day's drive, a long day's drive, what drinks to sip in which cafés. The restaurants we eat in are those he recommends.

So I feel myself a student once again. And I try to tell my daughters what it's like, effectively, to watch the world through other eyes, to live inside a book. "We know that already," they say.

A recommended "thing to do" is visit the Bories. This is a reconstructed village outside Gordes; we drive there one bright afternoon. The word *borie* comes from a Ligurian term meaning *cavity,* and these *cabanes gauloises,* or huts, dot the hillside of the plain of Clarapèdes. No one knows how old they are. They were inhabited in the nineteenth century and functional as dwellings long before. The cave of Sénancole, not half a mile away, was lived in in the neolithic period. Stone huts built without mortar are found throughout France—and in Ireland also, and Sardinia, and Mycenae, and the Yucatán.

They stand, on average, one story high. They rise straight up, and then there is corbeling and a false vault. The top is flat. The stones are slanted slightly so that the rain runs out, not in; where the corbeling begins, the stones are counterweighted; flagstones on top steady the whole. There is a chimney, a smoke hole, and often a sleeping story built on beams to take advantage of the chimney's warmth. The village is a cluster of such structures, five dwelling places and their outbuildings: a collective oven, storage units, shoemakers' huts, and silkworm factories. They bred and fed silkworms here.

Beyond, the land has been terraced. There used to

be olive, almond, and mulberry trees; only the olive remains. Low stone walls border the vines. Silkworms eat voraciously; the women of the village were kept busy stripping leaves. You could hear the silkworms eating, we were told, for miles; you could hear the shoemakers' hammers and the olive press.

It is a difficult place to describe—a haunted, hard, magical place. A local craftsman, Pierre Viala, spent eight years restoring the village. First he cut back undergrowth. Vines and earthquakes and tree roots had done damage, though a properly built *borie* will last a thousand years. Then Viala matched the tumbled rock, painstakingly determining which ruin matched with which. I have some sense of the achievement, since I sweated over dry-stone walls on our farm in upstate New York. I worked hard repairing them and acquired what appeared to be the rudiments of skill. There was satisfaction in the lift and heft and placement, in knowing that the border of a field had lurked within it jaggedly and could break the blades off plows. The stone boat and the mallet proved serviceable tools. When confident enough, I built my own free-standing dry-stone wall.

I set it—foolish, prideful choice—in view of the kitchen window, in front of a barbed-wire fence. Cows grazed beyond. There were willow trees, a stream, an incline; these were delights, not difficulties; I whistled while I worked. "It's beautiful," Elena said. I did not disagree.

As the manual suggested—*The Forgotten Art of Dry-Stone Wall Building*—I saved out the best stones for last. They supplied the facing; they were flat and long and fine. When the wall was finished, we brewed a pot of coffee and gazed at it admiringly, sipping, staring at the landscape and the mottled coloration of its new component, the long steep stretch and sweep, the pond, the barn, the sky. A Jersey cow approached. It was propitious, perfect, the necessary final touch. I ran to get my camera. The cow looked up, incurious. It nuzzled this new fence or breathed upon it merely; I was too busy focusing to see. And then the whole thing fell.

The *bories*—empty now, untenanted—seem like Uxmal or Stonehenge, a significant circle of stones. But this is likely misleading; farmers built with rock because there was a lot of it, and they had to clear that stony plain known as the *garrigue.* They knew how to work without mortar, knew how to counterweight. Shepherds still build dry-stone shelters in the hills. They lived inside these structures and buried and worshipped elsewhere. The material was not, like that of the Pyramids, say, brought from a distance or manufactured; what seems strange and magicked to us was sensible to them. When plague came you could close the gates and keep the sick at bay.

There must have been some comfort in the shared enclosure; in times of plague whole villages would huddle to the huts. Others locked plague victims in and chose to live outside. It did not work, of course. The rats and fleas passed indifferently, dispassionately, from one side to the other of the stone. God's scourge—*fléau de Dieu,* that leveler—paid no attention whatsoever to No Trespass signs.

We eat weekly at a restaurant called Le Paradou. It is family style, with tables set outside on a stone patio. Beneath, a brook meanders through a meadow; above, there is a cliff face, then the road. The owners are a family; the husband cooks and the wife acts as maître d'hôtel. Their daughters wait on tables; their young son pours water and wine. They make us, increasingly, welcome; by month's end, without our having to ask, they bring Andrea *pommes frites*.

One night we sit beside an elderly gentleman and his grandson. They converse in low tones, ceremonially, making the meal an occasion. They appear to have traveled some distance together. The grandfather has splendid manners; he carves his meat precisely, he pats his lips with his napkin before he speaks or drinks. He questions his grandson as to school, friends, sports, clothing, cousins; the boy is nine or ten and wearing glasses. Perhaps because I never had a grandfather who took me out alone to eat, I find myself admiring—coveting, even—their easy interchange. They laugh and chat and study photographs of bicycles and share a half bottle of wine.

Elena's grandfather meant much to her and was a constant presence in her youth. "Papaito" came from Asturias, then went to Cuba before 1900, then traveled to America and worked at the hatter's trade. An ardent socialist, he helped organize the hatters' union; he was a dandy, ramrod-straight, with a stickpin in his tie. When I met him the first time, he was well into his nineties; we had an interview. This took place on a park bench off the Grand Concourse in the Bronx. I was to meet them there, Elena said; she went to fetch her grandfather from his nearby apartment. He strutted down the hill, elbows high, carrying a walking stick, hat at a jaunty angle. He was every inch the upright gentleman taking his constitutional, his beautiful granddaughter two steps behind. She was his to give away, his manner suggested, or to withhold; he asked me a few questions in a heavy Spanish accent, not seeming to wait for the answers, incurious, polite.

What I remember of the interview is its conclusion, not substance; after twenty minutes, he signaled that I should leave. I stood, he stood, Elena stood; I went to get my car. I turned, however, a moment later to watch them walk up the hill. Papaito moved so slowly now he showed his full age, hobbling; he leaned on his stick, on her arm. He had staged his entrance, but there should have been a curtain for retreat.

The metaphoric flight from Troy, Anchises on Aeneas's back, is also a story of comfort. It can happen on the Concourse or at Le Paradou, the generations traveling, the companionable presences of those we have held high in arms now lifting us instead. More and more I find my father's gestures in my own; I study the menu as he did, I take the same ten-minute nap and tell impatient children, "Just a minute," while I hunt for my lost keys. The city burning, its buildings laid waste, beloved comrades slaughtered—all this may have been supportable for old Anchises, fleeing, because of the strong shoulders of his son.

Elena, shopping, is stopped in the Lourmarin open-air market by a man perhaps thirty years old. He has slick black hair and a pencil-thin moustache; he brandishes a clipboard and a questionnaire. He works for the Office of Development and Tourism, he says; the banks of the Durance have been underutilized. There are plans for enlarged use of the river. He has been conducting a survey and hopes she will respond. "It will only take three minutes."

"Forgive me, I'm not from these parts."

"Madame, that is clear. It's all the more reason I want your opinion; I don't require answers from the natives. *They* would not be tourists."

"I like it here," she says. "I don't see the need for development."

"Will you stand in the way of progress? Will you impede our history?"

"Impede?"

He clears his throat. He takes a pen from his ear. She agrees to join his survey, to not be an impediment. They retreat to the stone bench by the fountain. He sits. He asks her for her name, nationality, and age. I join them when he asks for her address. There is an eddy of paper and dust in the car park; doors slam.

What would be the optimal usage, he wants to know, for the proposed development? Would madame sail on the river or canoe on it or swim in it, does she like aquatic sports? The Durance is a cold stony trickle. At other times it floods. Would she play tennis on the banks, would she go fishing or rafting by preference; where would she like the parking facilities to be situated, please? He shows her a map of projected facilities: here the boathouse, here the restaurant and tennis courts, and here the parking structure for the fishermen and those thousands who will come to water-ski.

"But the river is dry," she protests.

"These are modern times. There are ways. We will make it a lake."

"*Le Parlement, le mistral, et la Durance sont les trois fléaux de la Provence,*" I say.

"*Monsieur?*"

"I don't remember who said it. But Parliament, the mistral, and this river are the three disasters of Provence."

"This is your husband?" he asks.

Elena tries not to offend him. She promises to read the questionnaire. He removes it from his clipboard and we look. There are pictures of swimmers, of boats. There are flow charts for traffic patterns over bridges not yet built. He must have a certain number of responses, he explains, or his day has been a failure and the project will languish and those who wish to sail or water-ski will have to travel elsewhere for the opportunity. Thus the hard-earned hope of tourism will fail.

We like the region very much, we say, we are contented tourists. "You are romantic," he says. His pants are blue, cuffs frayed.

"It is not necessarily romantic," I say, "to be suspicious of change."

His gaze wanders; he has written us off. His shirt is white, tie black. "You are conservative romantics, that is plain. *Ça se voit.*"

The fountain has two stone faces: grinning, bulbous

children with wide mouths. Moss coats the gargoyle tongues.

"I wish you well with the questionnaire." Elena puts a check in the box that represents horse racing. "But it is not proper to argue with those you survey."

"M'sieurdame." He stands. "I shall tabulate your response." A tall blond family in hiking shorts approaches. They may prove more suitable; he initials a fresh sheet.

IV

✳

1964

In the fall of 1963, I returned to London. I had spent my childhood there, and it was a plausible place to call home. I was twenty-one years old and trying on identities for size. My college friends were in New York, San Francisco, Washington, venturing out on careers. But I hoped to be a writer, and American writers cut eyeteeth in Europe, or used to, and anyway I wasn't sure which side of the Atlantic would prove native ground. Nor was I sure, in truth, if ground should be native or foreign, if the artist is more fruitfully anchored or adrift.

Beginner's luck had held. Harvard does prepare you for the world in this one crucial way: if you succeed within its walls, you assume that you will when outside. And the roulette ball had settled on my number, seemingly; the wheel was kind. I had an option for a novel in my pocket—a tale occasioned by that trip two years before to Greece—the blessing of my parents, and a network of support.

I worked some hours every day for my uncle and his partners in their gallery on Cork Street, by the Burlington Arcade. Roland, Browse & Delbanco occupied a narrow Queen Anne structure with four floors. The facing was black brick. I hopped up and down stairs ceaselessly, an errand-boy with an owner's last name, preparing to learn art as trade. I shared the partners' tea. I had biscuits in the afternoon and tea again. We went to other galleries, museums, private houses, lunch. It was an education: the auction rooms, the trip to Scotland on the trail of a Chinese watercolorist, the whiff of fraud and snobbery and the flavor of real expertise ("This brush stroke's wrong; that couldn't be right"), the continual kind welcome of my relatives in Hampstead, the frame makers, passionate collectors, the muddle of a storage bin with its discovered pearl among white peas.

But my attention was elsewhere; I wanted to write. I had a contract, after all, for pages left that morning in a rented room. I was living in Wetherby Gardens, near the Gloucester Road. The winter felt incessant, gray and wet. There was a cold-water sink in the room, a toilet down the hall. A shilling in the meter bought minutes worth of heat; I worked swaddled by blankets, in bed.

Dianne would be coming that March. She had dropped out of Sarah Lawrence and recorded her first album, with her sister, Laurie; she was well on the way to success. My copy of their first release was to wear thin with use, smooth with repetition; I knew its lines by heart. I had written some of them. I yearned for sun, for heat, for the actual skin of my darling instead of promotional photos. We planned to move, when she arrived, to France.

My father's closest childhood friend remained his friend for life. They had grown up in Hamburg together, inseparable neighbors. As Hitler came to power, Alexander Bech-stein—we called him, always, Alex—moved to France. It was he, two years earlier, who had told Paul and me what route to take and what to visit on our journey south. He was an architect and partner in a small, Paris-based firm. He also had a house near Grasse, in the foothills of the Alpes-Maritimes, at Magagnosc La Lauve. Those words meant little to me then—as did Châteauneuf-de-Grasse and Opio—but I still can see his pencil, his nicotine-stained fingers circling, snaking down the map.

I visited Alex whenever I could. He was a rakish, long-limbed man with bad teeth and thick auburn hair. He laughed and drank mineral water—a kidney had been dam-aged—and smoked Gauloises incessantly. His were exuber-ant, infectious ways; he drove a Citroën at breakneck pace, plied us with chocolates and cheese. We loved him from the start. My father and he were madcap children, he would assure us when we asked—and my brothers and I did ask, often. He regaled us with stories of narrow escapes, of pranks in stodgy Hamburg when they both were young.

Our mother, too, loved Alex. She, who could be so severe, grew girlish at his approach. Whenever we ar-rived in France—as we did, in my childhood, with some regularity—he would be there to welcome us. He bounded from the gate. He gathered us in his arms. He smelled of tobacco and soap. Our mother pulled us off. She linked her arm in his with a proprietary gladness; she scolded him, not meaning it, for his pell-mell antics; when we went out to-gether, she drank too much white wine.

For he was charm itself. When he chose to focus the light of his attention, all the room grew vivid. He commuted from Paris to Grasse. Alex thought nothing, in those years, of driving all night long. He would show up after breakfast, bearing flowers and perfume. He lived with his widowed white-haired mother, Annie, and a collection of cats. In repose, his face went grim. There were dark secrets whispered about unhappy love affairs, a common-law wife dying in an asylum. His health was poor. We worried; he waved concern away. He was for me—and for many others, particularly women—the spirit of romance.

During the Second World War, he had been interned in the south—distrusted, he would claim, by the French and the Germans and the Italians impartially. He described his long imprisonments as if they were a lark. What he most missed, he told me, winking, were his cigarettes, not girls. It was easier to get a girl than a Gauloise.

Then he worked as a gardener in Le Rouret. He worked at the harvest in Grasse. Refugees from many countries and conditions huddled in Provence; some of them had money and bought land. The land was cheap. One of the refugee women had known his family in Hamburg and Vienna; she made Alex welcome at her house.

Lilo Rosenthal was tall and sickly seeming, with reserves of strength. She would live into her nineties, pampering herself. She took the waters in Montecatini, the air in the Swiss Alps. Her husband was a banker from Vienna with sufficient foresight—before the Nazis came rampaging—to transfer a part of his fortune to the United States. He left Lilo, in his sixties, to marry her best friend. "I never loved you," he said. "I wanted the *verdammte* war to be over with, that's all."

So Alex labored, as both artisan and architect, on

restoring the Rosenthal *propriété*. It had a commanding view, hectares of old olive groves, and a sizeable *bassin*. The mayor of the village had lived there previously; when water was piped from the mountains, he routed it first through his land. There was lavender in abundance and collapsed stone walls.

The Rosenthals became agronomists. Lilo enjoyed the gardens and there was survival as well as profit in food. They occupied themselves with increasing the olive yield and deciding what sort of peach trees might flourish and which strain of jasmine to plant. Christian Dior, I heard, took sanctuary in the house. Alex—whistling, smoking, lanky in his thirties, and insouciant, I'm certain—slept in a *ruine* nearby that he would later restore.

By 1964 the place was very much restored, with a large central farmhouse, or *mas,* and a winding entrance drive. The stone walls were rebuilt. A caretaker's cottage, once the *ruine,* nestled under oak trees across *le grand bassin*. This cottage was for rent. Lilo Rosenthal was lonely and alone. Her only son had died of cancer; her ex-husband also had died. The former was a piercing grief, the latter—she told Alexander—overdue. She was well into her seventies and fierce. She lived six months in Manhattan and six months in Provence. She was not averse to company provided Alex vouched for it; she did not need the rental but would not refuse it either. Her old friend knew my father and my father wrote the check. She would welcome the young man.

When Dianne arrived, we took a train from London to Milan. There I collected a car. It was an Alfa-Romeo convertible, brand new and midnight blue. It had a Blaupunkt radio, ornamental wheels, and off-white leather seats. I have owned many cars by now but none that could rival this first one in terms of the pride of possession conferred; I have driven better cars but none that thrilled me more. I was twenty-one years old and headed for the Riviera. The girl in the passenger seat wore dark glasses, had long hair, and carried a guitar. The Alfa idled, waiting. It must be handled carefully, the salesman said, you have to break it in.

We set off, therefore, carefully. We reached the *autostrada* and turned south. I remember driving in the recommended range for RPM those first hours and miles; this meant that we were relegated to the right-hand lane. Our progress was cautious, speed slow. Volkswagens, Deux Chevaux, and ancient Fiats tore by. Workmen gestured at us jeeringly. I crept along the margin, fearful, tormented by trucks.

Night fell. The hills behind Genoa were dizzying, a gauntlet of dark curves. I kept both hands clenched on the wheel. My bravura ebbed and fled; I was a boy in a strange place, far from my parents and home. Dianne's last name on her passport was not the same as mine; would we be arrested when we stopped at a hotel? Where were the hotels? Why were we in Italy, and who on this bleak hillside would find us if we stalled? Could I prove, at customs, that the car's papers were in order; what was that high whine beneath us when I double-clutched?

At length we reached Ventimiglia, then Menton. It was eleven at night. We found a village somewhere near the water, found a hotel, found a room. I have studied the map since and driven that route often and cannot, no matter how thoroughly I hunt, find the place again. I remember the concierge. She wore a checked and pleated dress, had moustache-hairs, and was knitting. There was construction on the square outside—stone, then wire fencing, then a crane. The hotel was bright blue. At a table in the dining room, three old men played cards.

I parked the car beneath a street light, by itself, hoping its stark visibility would serve to keep it safe. We carried in our bags and the guitar. The bed was bad. Dianne sat by the window, writing, adressing a series of postcards; I fell asleep with a crash. Now, more than twenty years later, I won't pretend to remember my dreams, to know if there were auguries of happiness ahead or omens instead of the trouble.

We woke up that March morning to a brilliant winter sun. We were served café au lait and bread and ham and jam and cheese; the car waited chastely, intact. We found our way to the Moyenne, and then, ascending, to the Grande Corniche. It was an astonishment. The sea beneath, the cliffs above, the plane trees and villas and villages, the riot of color and ruckus of shape, the umbrella pines jutting from rock, the loud hurtling *camions*—what had frightened me in darkness elated us in light. We took down the convertible top. We had a lovely lunch. Our French sufficed. We followed the *carte Michelin,* then Alexander's scrawled directions to the house.

We took the *autoroute* through Cannes, then secondary roads through Mougins and Valbonne. We passed the planned retirement community of Castellaras. At a cross-roads with an olive mill we turned sharply left. There were signs for Châteauneuf-de-Grasse and Opio and Le Rouret and the Chapelle Saint Matthieu.

The entrance sign for Les Neiges d'Antan was small and hand-lettered, on wood. Like many other properties, it had a private name; such sobriquets reflect an owner's sense of style. This quotation from Villon proved apt, though "the snows of yesteryear" were scarcely obvious. There was snow on the crest of the Pré-Alpes, perhaps, but none in the valley below. Rather, Les Neiges evoked the elegiac flavor of the place and *temps jadis;* sheep grazed beneath the olive trees, and the meadow by the *mas* was mowed—as if Villon were still alive—not by machine but scythe.

The drive through the olive trees was steep. It was narrow, gravel bedded, with switchbacks serpentining, rising through the trees. No olive trees, apparently, had been sacrificed to progress; the entrance climb was stately, past terraced walls and urns. The urns were terra cotta, bulbous, cracked. One or two lay on their side; most stood as high as my head.

Lilo Rosenthal was waiting. She walked us through the house. It felt, on the instant, like home. It had been built of stone and stucco, with terra-cotta roofing tiles; the floors were red octagonal tile, and the inside walls off-white. There was dark-stained, worm-pocked wood as beaming, on the cabinets, and on the entrance doors. Downstairs there was a kitchen and dining room and living room with a fireplace that had been blocked off. "The forest fires," she explained. "This chimney empties underneath the oaks. Last winter we had fire here." She shrugged, her hands held out.

The second floor contained two bedrooms—one large, one little, and a bath. A thickly braided rope coiled as a kind of banister along the winding steps. There were roses on the south-facing wall, dark green shutters, and a balcony with French doors off the master bedroom. Standing there at dawn, I learned, by a trick of wintry light reflected, you could see the hills of Corsica. At night there were the lights of Cannes and, nearer, to the northwest, Grasse itself. If it was not embedded in mist or rain or heat-haze, you could see a slice of sea. When the mistral blew, if the shutters were not fastened tight, you saw everything: the desert, the Alpes-Maritimes, the Romans, Napoleon marching, Cézanne in a field full of rock.

Mme. Rosenthal was an imposing woman, tall and stooped. She handed me the key. She said "You must call me Lily" and invited us over for tea. She wore yellow trousers and a silk shirt with a floral pattern. Her jewelry was silver, and her bracelets matched her earrings and the pendant at her neck. Her hair was dark brown, meticulously coiffed, with just a streak of gray; reading glasses dangled from a cord. Her eyes were brown and green. Her torso thickened from what would have been prominent breasts; her legs were thin. When I said to Alex, later, that she must have been quite beautiful, he disagreed. "She's better now," he said.

"Sorrow has improved her. She was always too severe."

We pulled the beds together in the master bedroom, then unpacked. There were flowers on the tables; a coal fire burned in *la chaudière.* I would learn, though it took time, how to control that furnace; it would be a mystery solved. This unit occupied a corner of the kitchen, a squat silver machine providing both the heat of the house and its hot water supply. The bathtub was of the old-fashioned, upright rectangular type, with a sitting platform—rather like the bath wherein Marat, in David's painting, expires marmoreally.

Since Dianne liked to bathe and liked the water hot, I spent a good percentage of those first weeks learning how to stoke. You cleaned the ash. You laid a fire of wood and paper and opened all the dampers for full air. You added coal from the scuttle, slowly damping down. You filled the scuttle full again from the coalbin by the cistern back behind the house. If it had been raining, you used the auxiliary pile. You waited an hour and hoped. You could not fill the firebox until the fire took; you had to avoid, however, too thin a bed of coals. You cut and split the wood. You hoarded twigs. You took comfort from the smell, the film of gray dust everywhere, the hiss and clattering chatter of heat. At night, at manageable expense, you switched to the electrical backup; you grew familiar if not competent with holding tanks and valves and conduits and secondary systems in the *cave.*

Much of what we found there we found for the first time. There was a Pyrofax gas oven, for instance, and a refrigerator one-third the size of those we took for granted in our parents' homes. It sat on a tin table. A breadbox with protective mesh hung suspended in the kitchen; the telephone and reading lamp and pull-chain toilet each seemed strange. The *cave*—a thick-walled, low-roofed structure adjacent to the kitchen—held wood, coal, wine, potatoes, fruit, and tools. We left our raincoats there and stockpiled copies of the *International Herald Tribune* and *Nice-Matin*. The former burned better, I learned.

At five o'clock, we did report for tea. Since the afternoon was mild, we would be served *à l'abri* of the southern wall, beneath the *vieux platane.* Often, later, we would seek the shelter of the plane tree, but in March the tree was leafless and permitted the spring sun. Water gurgled steadily out of *le grand bassin.* The patio was flagstone and the flower borders full. The dark green metal table—the same green as the shutters—had a tablecloth clipped to its top. There were three green metal chairs.

We sat and made conversation. Mme. Rosenthal—"Do call me Lily"—rang a bell. "These are my treasures," she said. Then, for their benefit, she repeated this in French: *"Ce sont mes trésors."* The man was in a coverall, the woman in a smock. His face was angular, intelligent, hers broad and smiling broadly. They bore trays. There was wine and Dubonnet and tea and biscuits and fruit. They set the table deftly, and we stood.

I am of average height, and Dianne tall. I know what it feels like to feel undersized, to be in the presence of adults when young or two hundred pound six-footers when adult.

But I have never known such perfectly proportioned folk as Guillaume and Felicity Levasseur who nonetheless were minuscule. They barely reached my shoulder, barely topped five feet.

"My little people," Lily said. *"Mes gardiens."*

"Your fire is in order?" Guillaume inquired. "You are tired from the trip?"

"You have what you require?" asked Felicity. *"Tout ce qu'il faut?"*

They did not speak and would not learn a single phrase of English. Through the years of friendship that would follow from this meeting, they cackled at and corrected my French, diligently teaching me until at length I heard no shift in rate or emphasis when they spoke to each other instead. But I could not return the favor. "He's too old and I'm too stupid," said Felicity. "It is not for us to understand these things."

In the presence of madame they were subservient, correct. We called her Lily by the second glass; she was *"la patronne"* in private, "madame" in public for the Levasseurs forever. They had recently arrived. This was their first position in the serving class. They had been visiting a cousin, and Guillaume's migraine headaches were a problem, truly, and he was too enervated to continue working in the shop. Felicity also preferred the full air. She had had tuberculosis when a child and had been sequestered in a sanitarium near Gréolières, and therefore she credited this part of the country—"It is not, however, *mon pays à moi,* you understand, not where we come from truly"—with having been restorative to health.

They were *maladif,* not strong. "As you see, we are

not large." She was the youngest of eleven children, and seven already had died. They had to pay attention to these matters, and the cousin with a heart condition liked it in the region and assured them they would too. The cousin knew the gardener at Les Neiges d'Antan. Mme. Rosenthal was strict but fair; she would not be unreasonable in her expectations and would be precise. Therefore they decided to move. They had accepted this position for the beauty of the *paysage,* the excellence of their accommodation on the third floor of the house, the six months' worth of privacy when *la patronne* was in New York, the providential lack of winters such as those they suffered in the Massif Central.

I learned all this later, of course. That afternoon they were discreet—efficient, bustling in the service of the visitors, since *les jeunes gens* would certainly be tired from the trip. The necessaries—bread, wine, cheese, pâté, butter, coffee, lettuce, eggs—had been purchased, and tomorrow they would show us where to shop. Were the beds sufficient? Was the heating system clear? Might they help us with the bags or wash the car? If there was anything we needed we had but to ask.

Lilo was impatient; she required center stage. She wanted news of Alex Bechstein, and her sister knew my uncle, and the name of Dianne's father was not unknown to her either. She wondered what we knew of Joan of Arc. She had been studying the history of Joan of Arc and was a photographer: not professional—she made a deprecatory gesture, she poured a second *infusion*—but not quite an amateur either. She was engaged in photographing the birthplace of Joan of Arc and the sites of her brief triumphal progress through France. The year before she did the same with Roman roads. She would show us her album of bridges and aqueducts and amphitheaters and the remaining roadways in Provence. They were remarkable, the Romans, and so was Joan of Arc.

The Romans had a sameness, a pedestrian consistency, *n'est-ce pas;* they did not respond to the particularities of place. To the Roman legions or the legion of their engineers it was a matter of indifference if they conquered Britain, Switzerland, or France. The subject populace and landscape would be treated much the same. The model for the baths would be unchanged. They were like the English in the days of Queen Victoria: no adjustment must be made to native ways. The English—have you noticed?—speak with perfect fluency and no concession whatsoever to the niceties of accent; it would be a moral failing to inflect.

I was a writer, was that not correct? I should pay attention to the problems of a region in such flux. When she settled in these hills there had been no motor cars worth mentioning, nothing to disturb a way of life that had gone undisturbed for centuries before. That graveyard for tires by *le moulin,* those motorcycles everywhere, the tourist buses up from Cannes, these factories emitting poison in the service of perfume—I should pay attention to the wreckage in the valley while there still was something of its ancient ways to see.

We thanked her; she pushed back her chair. A wind arose. Felicity returned with trays; we thanked her also and withdrew. It had been a long day. The fire needed tending. I fiddled with it haplessly till Guillaume arrived with coal. We cooked what they had bought for us, two children playing house.

Soon after our arrival, Lilo left. The rains did not agree with her; she had matters to attend to; she would return at April's end and stay till it grew hot. We drove about, exploring; we found markets and museums. We walked the local roads. On the southern side of the valley, in a grove of cyprus, a mausoleum rose. The widow who erected it had willed her property and house to the indigent insane. Two hundred scenic hectares were therefore exempt from development; glass shards had been embedded on top of the stone walls.

In order to earn extra cash, Guillaume delivered gas tanks to the mountain villages—Coursegoules, Gréolières, Gourdon. Sometimes I went too. We left in the cold pre-dawn dark, at five o'clock. His gray Renault would choke and sputter into life, and slowly we ascended where the rain-slick curves turned icy and then had been covered with snow. He rarely got out of first gear. The heater did not work; the motor whined and howled. We followed larger trucks, sprayed by the wake of their wheels. Then it grew light. We collected empty canisters and replaced them with the full. *"Vous allez vous salir, ce n'est point nécessaire.* You'll make yourself dirty," Guillaume would protest. *"Mais non,* it isn't necessary." Nonetheless, warming, I helped.

The *patron* of the hotel or restaurant or café would always offer coffee, and always we accepted. Guillaume and the *patron* would discuss the weather, berating it, beating their arms. Then we would descend, less heavily laden, braking, looking at the river Loup like an ice channel underneath, and far away the sea. The snow turned back to rain.

I would return at eight o'clock, to Dianne still asleep, to radiators popping and a cat within the bin.

Alexander came to visit; my aunt and uncle from London came too. We discovered restaurants in Haut-de-Cagnes and Saint-Paul-de-Vence and Antibes; we ballooned on *boules* and croissants and pâté and olives and cheese. We rambled through the flower markets in Grasse and Cannes and Nice, buying armfuls of anemones. We cut the bright mimosa that bloomed beside the house; we gathered tulips, irises, and daisies from the fields. We waited for the figs to ripen on the fig tree, for the peaches and the cherries and the pears. We went to Vallauris and the Madoura pottery and the Grimaldi Museum and the Picasso and Léger museums and the Musée Fragonard.

A friend from college came to visit; we played cards. We entertained the Levasseurs, and they invited us to picnic in the olive groves. We learned the butcher's name. The grocer commended that afternoon's fruit, and the lady at the post office grew affable; we discussed the weather with her daily, returning from the bakery with bread. We greeted the gardener's wife; she was fine-featured, reticent, and would raise her hand in answer while her husband doffed his cap. He was a drunkard, we heard; his family had once owned much land in the region. Felicity loved gossip. She dropped her voice and tilted her face forward and confided that the mayor was reputed to be keeping an *algérienne* in Grasse. He was sleeping, also, with that redhead in the *tabac*. Guillaume demurred. "It's not certain," he would tell me, "it's only what they say." When the *patronne's* away, the mice will play the radio at night; they were saving to buy a TV.

I rose with the first light and stoked the stove. I made coffee for myself and ate a biscuit and sat down to work. As spring progressed I wrote outside, by the climbing roses and the bittersweet. My book accreted, paragraph by page; I broke off when Dianne woke up. She descended catlike, stretching, absorbed by her dark dreams. She rubbed the sleep-sand from her eyes and turned on France-Musique.

We planned the day. We visited *parfumeries* or circled Cap d'Antibes. While the Alfa-Romeo was being serviced, twice, we passed the time in Cannes. We wandered through the old port and ate oysters and took a ferry to the near Iles de Lerins. We sang and gestured at each other as if indeed we were a pair of star-crossed theatrical lovers. The ending would be sad. "Sail away," the sailors chorus; it says so in the script. *"Matelot, matelot,* where you go my heart goes with you; *matelot, matelot,* when you go down to the sea."

We drove to Barcelona, following the coast. We stopped in Saint-Tropez and ate again at Baumanière—this time I knew not to order contradictory tomatoes, and our midnight-blue convertible could hold its own—and saw the gypsies gathering at Les Saintes-Maries-de-la-Mer. We spent a night in Collioure and time in Cadaqués and, finally, Barcelona. Dianne's grandmother was Spanish, and she had just died. Dianne sat weeping in the Ritz about the loss of her beloved mother's mother and how the woman at the table to our right reminded her of what she would not see alive again: uncritical devotion, unwavering support.

Some military dignitary spoke at the hotel, and there were soldiers everywhere. Guards patrolled the halls. I think I knew in Barcelona (more than when she left Les Neiges, when I took her to the airport, when we left each other, later, in Martha's Vineyard and Manhattan with brutal regularity) the sordidness of loss, the self-deception of a backwards look, and that it would not work. She huddled in our bedroom, weeping; we returned to Châteauneuf-de-Grasse as if it were a stay against confusion. But she did not stay.

Often, in the years to come, I wondered what went wrong. It was a difficult time. We were not ready for marriage, and that would have been the logical next step. Dianne became allergic to the local wine. She did not know it then, and we drank unstintingly, and every night she lay and shook and worried over what to do and if she should go home. Our two beds matched, but they were single, and we called the space between them *"le grand trou."* This was a joking reference to the "big pit" behind the woodshed where Guillaume piled and burned the garbage every other day; we dumped our coal ash also, and it smoldered there.

But *le grand trou* would widen, though we visited each other in the beds. We disagreed about the way to wash the coffee cups and where to stack the plates. She was homesick for her mother and her sisters and her brother; I thought I should be family sufficient, all she'd need. We had pointless arguments about the way to share a future—pointless since I think we knew that it would not be shared. Her record proved successful beyond all expectation; a cut from that first album was climbing *Variety's* chart. And her producer and manager wanted her back in New York. They urged her, not unreasonably, to take advantage of the interest aroused. They offered café bookings and a concert tour and a second album; I offered goat's cheese and my silent self-absorption and a paragraph a day.

"They want me back," she said.

"Who's they?"

"The producer. The A&R man. Laurie."

"Laurie can wait. She knew you were leaving."

"We're in this together," she said.

"And where does that leave me?"

"You could come too."

"And carry your guitar again? And sit there in The Bitter End until the bitter end again? No thanks."

"I'm not going, really. I'm just going home. I have to do this."

"Why?"

"Because I started it. We started it. We promised each other we'd try."

"How long?"

"A year. It's not too much to ask."

"It isn't, no. It's more than I was asking."

"It's lonely here. It isn't working."

"No."

The rest is quickly told. Our edges grew jagged, mismatched. I think I knew or guessed that writing is a private business, performance by definition public. Still, it's one thing to perceive incompatibility and another to live through it. *"Partir, c'est courir un peu."*

The Levasseurs were kind. Lilo Rosenthal returned, and we came to know each other better, a process that continued in the years to come. I flew to Greece to verify some sites and street names for my book, then prepared to return to New York. The travel agent at American Express in Cannes was helpful and exact. He told me of a ferry in Le Havre, its departure times and bills of lading, how to ship the car.

Solitary now, I drove the length of France. The *autoroute* seemed simple to negotiate; Fiats, Volkswagens, and Deux Chevaux hugged the right-hand lane. I arrived in Le Havre elated, exhausted, and found my way to the dock. There was a fine mist rising; whistles blew. The ferry had been discontinued eighteen months before.

V

✳

1987

This summer, with our two children in tow, I remember a brief visit with my parents and my younger brother, Andrew, to Provence. It was 1965. I had been an intern at the United Nations in Geneva, attending a conference with the improbable topic—for me—of "Rural Development in Africa." I stayed in Grand-Saconnex and dabbled in diplomacy, learning that it also would not prove a career. As with the art gallery in London, my thoughts were elsewhere, vague. I listened to the speeches and the static in the headset, drifting off. So routine a waste of words must trouble any language-lover, devaluing the currency of speech.

My parents and my thirteen-year-old brother had been traveling in Europe; I met up with them in Rome. We rented a car and traversed the Italian and French Rivieras, stopping in those places where I could play guide. This was not easy. My mother was proud of her accentless French and supervisory. In high school, when I studied conjugations, I remember reciting: *"Naquit. Il naquit."* She hooted with laughter, *"Est né. Il est né.* That's what you really mean. Nobody uses that form of the past. Nobody gets born that way, except perhaps in books."

My father left for a business meeting; the weather

was brutally hot. The little shops and long *allées* felt totemic, hard to share. The museums and hill villages had lost their power to engage attention; the Croisette appeared vulgar, not chic.

Fire threatened the Red Rocks and much of l'Est-érel; the flying fire engines dipped and spat. Propeller planes flew back and forth above us, collecting water and releasing it, airborne tank by tank. This did not seem likely to work. Though we met Alex Bechstein at La Colombe d'Or, eating in the garden, by the Miró mosaic, he appeared unwell. We ordered *loup*, the wolffish from the nearby river; he toyed with it, distracted. He spoke of a small structure he had bought in Magagnosc, a new *ruine* to renovate: a pigeon house.

That night we stayed in a château on the outskirts of Vence. My mother had expensive tastes. "We are not rich enough," she liked to say, "to buy anything but the best." So our hotel was elaborate—the porters hushed yet supercilious, the furnishings ornate. The French when lavish yield to none in their prideful pretension; I found it hard to sleep.

"It is only in France one eats well," she confided to her travel journal. "Interesting talk with Alex." What, I wonder—but it is gone past recovery—did they discuss when alone? Did they speak of disappointment or realized hopes or youthful aspiration or sit in companionable silence, smoking, or wonder—as I do, today—how they had come to this pass?

At midnight I went for a walk. The sky was clear. D. H. Lawrence died in Vence, and Matisse survived there to design the Rosaire Chapel. There is a time for the grand tour, a time for first love on the loose. If one be fortunate enough, there is a season for sports cars and parental help and sojourns at the Ritz. But one must turn—one cannot help the turning, or be doomed to repetition—away from "childish things." I was twenty-two years old. I was full of self-pity and pride and even then, I think, a kind of anticipatory nostalgia. It washed over me that night in the dewy gardens of the château; it has colored this account. Smoke spiraled a hillside away, its diffusion visible. A flying fire engine droned above.

The neighbors' dog has the run of our house. He is a toy poodle, snippy and pert, spoiled in the way the French coddle their pets; they provide him a pillow, the best bits of meat. They give him continual grooming, applaud his two tricks. He yaps and nips and leaps. He enters our front door at will, making for the kitchen. What he particularly likes is to drink from the downstairs bathtub—a sunken, marbled rectangle—then pee.

Our neighbors have moved here from Paris. He is a retired engineer, she—his second wife—an art historian. They share a love of music, opera by choice. Every night they sit on the porch, drinking, listening to Mozart or Puccini, admiring Neil the dog. Their sound system is good. Once or twice they have asked us to join them, and we drink cognac or coffee and sit in the windy darkness, listening to *"Un bel di"* and *"La ci darem."*

Mme. LaBecque is a specialist in Provençal painting

of the fourteenth and fifteenth centuries; she works at the Granet Museum in Aix. She speaks of *"l'art de la région"*— its great flowering, its slow collapse, its relatively few extant examples. You can tell a Provençal portrait, she says, by the shadow that the figures cast; there's always sunshine in a painting, even if the figure stands inside a room. There is a quality of brightness to the light.

Her husband is proud of her. He nods his white head approvingly while she tells me of the masters who made Avignon their base. He is pleased, he tells me, to be able to afford their home, to water his garden and listen to music and let his knowledgeable spouse pursue researches in Aix. A daughter by his first marriage lives in Cleveland, and I show him—on the tablecloth—the distance between Cleveland and Ann Arbor, then the distance between Cleveland and other cities with which he is familiar, San Francisco and Boston and New Orleans. "New York of course also," he says. He lifts his hands, then drops them—a dismissive gesture. "Everybody knows New York."

The dog is their baby, their joy. He can roll on his back and then beg. When he cocks his head, surveying the table, they praise his rapacious attention. He is musical, they say, except that he dislikes Wagner; every time we put on Wagner, especially a heldentenor, Neil wants to leave the room. Elena says that her father had a cocker spaniel called Missy who howled at a particular passage in the Victor Herbert cello concerto; she would hear it on the radio and be inconsolable. *"Les cockers,"* says our host. *"Elles sont mignonnes.* They are charming. But they have very sensitive ears."

When we leave at night (or in the morning, watching him direct her as she backs their car onto the hill, waving as she sputters down the steep incline to Lourmarin, or while they water the garden together, or settle on the patio for lunch), I find myself imagining the *troisème âge,* retirement, in just such a context as this. They play cards with the deaf general across the road. They read the papers aloud, impatient with but grudgingly impressed by Mitterrand. They are interested, to a point, and to a point indifferent as to the price of oranges, the demographics of Spain. They pay close attention to Neil the poodle and Mozart and cognac and flowers; they appear wholly content. When I ask my neighbor—taking the traveler's privilege of sudden if spurious intimacy—if he is in fact contented, he says, *"Ma certo, como no!"* as if such a sentiment could not be ventured in French. "Of course," he tells me, departing, "of course I am happy. Relieved. You understand me, yes?"

I understand him, yes, I say, and then he says something surprising. "The thousand and one nights, remember"—he winks—"that remarkable history of Scheherazade. *Vous comprenez,* Nicholas—the perfect romancer, the perfect romance, the poet's talkative muse. It did not last three years."

Petrarch first glimpsed Laura in a church in Avignon. This is well recorded by the poet himself: on April 6, 1327, in the church of Sainte-Claire, he found his muse. The Canzonière ensued. Begun in 1330, they consist of three hundred and seventeen sonnets, twenty-nine canzoni, nine sestinas, seven ballads, and four madrigals. Laura died—on April 6 again—in 1348, most probably of the plague.

Petrarch detested Avignon but liked Fontaine-de-Vaucluse. There he retreated, often, between 1337 and 1352, to phrase his courtly fancy by the waters of the Sorgues. A museum in the little town displays a collection of portraits of Laura. Her face changes with the painter, and we know little about her in incontestable fact. Laura de Sabran, Laura du Thor, Laura Colonna, and Laura de Caumont have been serially proposed as imagination's original; she has as many guises as the sonneteer's "dark lady," though she comes to us in white. Most plausibly she was the wife or daughter of a man called Paul de Sade, or so insisted the Abbé de Sade and, later, the Marquis.

I like that lineage best. It's fine to think the author of *Justine* should be related to a woman "remarkable for her virtue," Petrarch's chaste ideal. The marquis himself liked the notion; he wanted to keep Laura's ashes secure in a family vault. His ruined castle at Lacoste is an easy drive (and would have been a hard day's ride) from Fontaine-de-Vaucluse. Though marquis of the region for thirty years, he lived in it for only four.

De Sade's castle on the hill looks scarcely more inviting than the rock-wreckage of the *bories*. Still, it is being restored. Boys and girls with wheelbarrows carry in cement; they must cross some planking laid across a ditch. The ditch was once a moat, no doubt, and there may be method in all of this rearranged rubble. Yet the task—to cite another author of the region—looks Sisyphean, thankless at best; it is a big hill and a heavy rock and the labor less than skilled. Again it seems something de Sade would enjoy: all these sun-scorched children sweating in his honor, smoking, sharing tents.

Albert Camus made his home in Lourmarin because of the size of the sky. It reminded him, apparently, of Algeria. He wanted to be anonymous, or tried to be, sitting in the café with an invented name—smiling, nodding, affable, a man of the people, the people would say. His address is in the phone book still; he is buried not a mile from where we stay. In the village cemetery there are mausoleums everywhere, plastic flowers and photographs of the beloved and sculptured likenesses and marble bibles: the paraphernalia of sentiment and grief, men watering rosebushes, their mothers at their feet. So Camus's grave is all the more moving, with its ancient-seeming stone and no inscription other than his name. Lavender grows thickly as its only decoration. His wife's stone matches; they lie unremarked.

Heat at midday; then thunder and rain. There is something self-consciously simple about the poets of this place: Jean Giono, for instance, and even Mistral and his Félibriste crew. (Like those who "antique" new furniture by drilling wormholes in. Or build a ruin purposively so as to make the view historical, or write with a quill pen.) Alphonse Daudet supposedly wrote his *Letters from My Windmill* from a windmill in Fontvieille. In fact he wrote it in Paris, at a civilized remove. But the windmill is now a museum, and there are photographs. Daudet sits *au Mas de Vers en Camargue* on a straight-backed chair, smoking, sporting his black hat. Frédéric Mistral sits next to him, in an armchair; their feet are hidden by high grass. Mistral is in a light suit and a vest and is holding what appears to be a walking stick or cane. The men are posed, lugubrious.

They do not pretend to conversation or amusement; their sightlines do not meet. Daudet looks slightly younger. Mistral sits closer to the camera and is therefore enlarged. Daudet's moustache and side-whiskers are dark, Mistral's goatee has gone white. What these chairs are doing in the field is anybody's guess.

In the upstairs portion of the mill, the wall has a circle of names. They are the thirty-two winds of Provence; their names, the ticket-taker cautions, are not French but Provençal. She has taken insufficient tickets; she is bored this afternoon. "You'd be surprised," she tells me, "how many people come here for the mill and don't know there's a museum downstairs. *Bien des gens.* Often they are unaware that we have artifacts. *Lettres de mon moulin,* for example, was translated into Esperanto and Chinese. I am certain you didn't know that. Also the *Contes du Lundi.*"

But if the museum devoted to Petrarch be a modern house, the windmill a museum, and the castle in Lacoste bear no resemblance now to that of the marquis, the Fontaine-de-Vaucluse itself is very much the same. Water still comes spewing out of the rockface, its throat full of rivers too deep for discovery, its underground cavern unplumbed. Men have dived to record depths and not gone to the bottom; they have sent down robots, and the robots—faced with openings too narrow to maneuver—have turned back. So where the water comes from, and what it looks like, gushing forth, is a question the poet continues to pose, a picture still to be drawn. What Petrarch saw we see. His friend Simone Martini, while in Avignon, illustrated Petrarch's copy of Virgil; Virgil too would have found in the Sorgues a subject fit for evocation in the ancient way. We have been imitating one another's imitations since we first held the mirror to nature and saw ourselves refracted in the pool.

The names of the great troubadours are themselves a song: Bernard de Ventadour, Marcabrun, Bertran de Born, Guillaume IX de Poitiers. This last-named was first-born, in 1087; Giraud Riquier, "the last of the troubadours," died in 1294. There were Pèire Cardenal, Guilhem de Montanhagol, Guiraud de Calanson, and Folquet de Marseille. Jauffré Rudel was of that company, as were Bernart Marti, Rigaud de Barbezieux, Raimon de Miraval, and the Comtesse de Die. There were Raimbaud de Vaquerias and Pèire d'Alvernhe, and Guillem de Cabestanh.

So the bards took root and flower in Provence. It is not, at first sighting, a landscape for men with lutes and plumes and sonnets to their mistresses' eyebrows; it looks both too bright and severe. M. F. K. Fisher, who writes of the region with sweet knowingness, finds Les Baux malevolent. Dante appears to have used it as the landscape for his hell. He had once considered writing the *Commedia* in Provençal; he wanted to tip his troubadour's cap to *"il miglior fabbro,"* the better maker, Arnaut Daniel.

This time we do not stop to eat at L'Oustau de Baumanière. We climb the steep switchbacks in traffic. The court of Les Baux, where poetry flourished, feels anything but courtly now; it costs seven francs to enter town and fifteen to get past the shops. There is a gate and entrance fee and revolving turnstile. The crest of the hill has been left unretouched, but the low streets are a hive of commerce—olive-wood sculptors and jewelers and cafés and boutiques. The court itself is a dismantled rock pile: steps, a parapet remaining, half a roof. From this height you can see swimming pools in all four directions, then the valley full of bauxite, which takes its name from the town. Lizards flicker, sunning. A monument stands at cliff's edge to the peasant-poet who "sang this land," Charloun Rieu.

On market day in Arles it proves difficult to park. The car inches forward. Women with shopping bags easily outdistance us on foot. At length we come upon a space and walk towards the market; men selling flowers call to us, as do children with chickens and bread. The vendors themselves are a crowd. They sell leather and Indonesian jewelry and a red powder guaranteed to cure all ills, from arthritis to neuralgia of the teeth. They proffer books on medicinal cures. A plastic snake lies coiled beneath a plastic bubble, and a sign proclaims, "Not miracle but fact. You are your own best healer. This cures cancer of the liver, impetigo, ringworm, and phlebitis. It is the ancient way!"

We examine combs and knives and wallets; we pass whole stalls devoted to soap. Some vendors specialize in lavender, honey extract, and herbes de Provence; others offer scarves and belts and screwdrivers and tape. In the distance someone practices a flute; ahead, a saxophonist stumbles through "Blue Moon." A thin boy with wire spectacles works through the D-minor cello suite by Bach. His modern cello is blond, its case open at his feet. I put in sufficient money so that he nods, blinking, and misses a phrase.

They sell live poultry and puppies and pizza and fish. There are stalls for hats—the black, traditional ones of Provence and straw boaters and sailor's caps. By the gardens of the amphitheater (the posters here proclaim that *Tosca* was in town last night, Fats Domino the night before) a man sells flintlock pistols and elaborately decorated swords. He wears a gray ponytail and leather clothes; the girl at the next stall has the hard-scrubbed beauty and the face of "L'Arlesienne." Germans in quantity file past, and Americans and Dutch. "Have you seen the Alyscamps?" I hear. "It's a very definite must."

A girl tries on a brocade belt and sucks in her stomach, then exhales with a rush. The attendant shakes his head. Men sell ice cream and cold drinks. A fire engine, its klaxon blaring, beats past. "And that place van Gogh went mad, Saint-Rémy. The place that he cut off his ear, it's amazing what they've got there now. A bridge just like the one he painted." We advance to the cheese and fish.

How can they sell enough watches and charms; what makes it worth their while? The trinket trays remain full at noon; the statuettes of Sarah and the gypsy dancers and the three Marys from Les Saintes-Maries-de-la-Mer and the Provençal drummer, his fife in his mouth, and the tire irons and flashlights and sets of metric wrenches get taken up and packed away and driven off in vans.

At noon they shut the stalls. Refrigerated fish trucks drive away. The old man with his radishes and fennel folds his chair. Those who came to buy their lunch are gone to start preparing it; those who plan to eat in restaurants are planning where to eat. We have bought three kinds of olives, a pair of plastic wraparound sunglasses for Andrea, pasta with basil, and ten honey-scented bars of soap. A woman with luxuriant moustachios walks past, and a man without arms. Those ducks that were not purchased will survive till next week's market; those plump enough to be selected have had their necks already wrung.

An art show takes place in the Lourmarin Foyer Rural—a contest for local painters, with a prize. Elena and I step inside to glance at what is hanging there, and the blond lady at the desk hands us each a piece of paper, then tells us to mark down the number of the artist we prefer. There are twenty-five entrants, with a limit of three pictures each; most have submitted two.

It is the usual collection of amateurish kitsch: blue cypress trees, white steeples, a fluffy set of kittens tugging fluffy balls of yarn. Clouds hang suspended in perfect blue skies, and the cliffs of Roussillon receive sustained attention. Landscape predominates here. Perhaps the contest stipulates that the entries must be realistic, depicting local landscape—but that seems unlikely; there are a few half-hearted stabs at abstraction and a design or three. Winston Churchill painted these scenes; there is a photograph, in the château, of the great man plumply perched in front of his easel and view. He sojourned often in Aix, and drove up to the Lubéron to paint. Picasso said, apparently, that Churchill could have made a living with the brush. How far his tongue was in his cheek we do not know.

One or two of the entrants have talent; one of them, particularly, conveys the sun-struck dapple of village square and tree. His figures have authority and verve. Elena and I cast our votes. The pictures are for sale. His prices are modest, and I ask, casually, of the blonde at the door if they have shipping arrangements. This is a mistake. She is delighted, voluble. She herself is a painter and has had a show, her husband is a doctor in the region, she is Polish and has relatives in Detroit. There are difficulties with customs, *les douanes*. France owns every painting and they make complications even if you are a foreigner; the minister of justice, it appears, must determine if what you are taking is treasure and irreplaceable.

I mention Douanier Rousseau. Is it not ironic that customs, which once gave that great painter Henri Rousseau his nickname and his livelihood, now provides an obstacle to painters? "So you know about these things," she says, and we are invited to meet the artist, to telephone, to see the atelier. We shake hands with another woman, who has organized the space. Our problem is particular; we will leave before the exhibition finishes, before the judging, even, and we could not therefore legitimately take away the picture. But it can be arranged. I say that we will think about it, we must collect our children, thank you very much. She herself has two children, aged fourteen and twelve; she hopes that we will come again this afternoon. She does not agree with our choice of the winner but will present our compliments nevertheless. "Reflect on it," she says. We promise to reflect on it and make our escape.

The car, however, has been blocked. A little beige van with Police on its door is double-parked behind me; a stone wall looms in front. I look inside the pharmacy to see if there's a uniform; the pharmacist says, no, he isn't here. I should consult the post office; she will do it for me happily. Brigitte in the post office has not seen him either; *tiens,* they say, he's always doing this, what an extraordinary man. I have never seen a policeman in town and therefore would not know him. He is perhaps next door, at the Crédit Agricole. They give me his name. I inquire at the Crédit Agricole. *"C'est moi-même,"* says a man at the desk, "That is myself." I explain the trouble with the car; we both apologize. He completes his transaction and hurries out; he backs up, permitting our exit and blocking the next car instead.

At the Cave Cooperative we fill our plastic flagons with the local red and white. You can buy containers of five or ten or twenty liters, returning them when empty; they fill these *bonbons* with a hose. The girl who turns the spigot and then writes up the transaction has grown friendly over time. She says, "You come from Lourmarin, so I just write *à pied.* I will say you came 'on foot.' I should properly write down your car license number, because of the police. But for Lourmarin it isn't worth the trouble; he won't arrest you, certainly."

I mention that I just made the acquaintance of the police. "Yes," she says. "I saw him this morning. And I was driving with some speed and did not have my seatbelt on. You know, it's necessary now in France to fasten *la ceinture*. But he smiled and waved at me; he's not concerned, that one; it's all right to mark, here, *à pied.*"

There is a place to rent horses out by the Hôtel de Guilles. Ten horses are tethered in town. Five men and five women drink beer and coffee and pastis at the Café Ollier beside the fountain; it is not difficult to match them with the horses. The men wear T-shirts and hats. Their skulls are shaved. They have full beards, however, and the effect is startling, systematic; there is the edge of menace to them, though they joke and laugh. Their leader, the one with the gray beard and cigar, studies a map. He folds and unfolds it and points. The women are younger, athletic. One horse tugs free and wanders off, and a girl like an arrow retrieves it and ties the reins, not gently, to the bumper of a car.

The horses shit. There are flies. Perhaps I have watched too many Westerns, too many versions of *The Outlaws Come to Main Street,* but these bearded, nodding men and their compact girls in jeans seem jarring and discordant. *"Muchacha."* A town boy whistles. *"Fräulein.* Baby. Come *on."* I have seen him pumping gas. He is trying out his languages. The man with a cigar points it in the boy's direction and says, softly, decisively, "Pop."

The woman from the gallery has informed herself. Beneath a certain price, and as long as the artist is living, there are no difficulties. The difficulty is only that of expedition and the deadline of the show and the judging; after all, and though she should not reveal such knowledge, our particular entry has received two first-prize votes. She would not willingly betray the secret of the ballot box, but in this particular case . . . I tell her a story I have heard about Picasso. He gave a splendid dinner party in an expensive restaurant; his friends ate well, and much, and long. Picasso enjoyed himself hugely. When the waiter brought him the hugely commensurate bill, he turned it over, scribbled some lines—a sketch, a signature—and offered, "Keep the change."

A family plays *boules* in the increasing dark. The father and his son and what appears to be a cousin play on one team; the wife, the grandfather, the cousin's husband on the other. The father is fierce and instructive. Each time the boy releases a ball he gets lectured about his mistakes. "More height, more length, more wrist," the father calls. *"O là, la vâche."*

    "Leave him alone," the grandfather says. "He's doing as well as he can."

"I want him to do better. *Don't* pick up your ball, stupid, not till it's over, not till you know exactly where it ends. Everything can change."

The lecture continues. The boy takes it well. The mother grows impatient; they play beneath the streetlamp's light, the father keeping score and track and a running commentary on his son's mistaken ways. What makes this notable, however, is that the boy consistently betters his elders; he is easily the best of them, and knows it, and they do too.

That night there is a concert in the Foyer Rural. Walking past the open door, on our way for ice cream and coffee, we hear a guitar. The poster announces that Marcel Raynaud and his chorus of children will sing songs of "friendship and faith." Admission is free. The picture on the poster shows an affable man with guitar, staring soulfully up at the camera; he wears a sports jacket and tie. The doorway is ill lit, the night dark. There is the first crescent of moon. The guitar sounds accurate, the voice inside plaintive yet clear; we stand in the back, then sit down.

On our first night in Lourmarin, there had also been a program in the Foyer Rural. We arrived too late and hungry, however, to attend; it had been a snake-charming show. The posters then—less affable—proclaimed that we might see the only man in Europe who could kiss a cobra, the single Western man on intimate terms with his snake.

He charmed tarantulas also, and a boa constrictor like a feathered boa was wrapped around his neck. *Entrée* was twenty francs. The boa had been highlighted, red.

On our way back from dinner, then, we paused to admire the sign. A girl approached. I had noticed her, before, in the lit doorway of the Foyer, because of her bright hennaed hair. She untied the sign from its post. She was holding others in the hollow of her arm. I said it looked impressive, that we regretted missing the display; she said we could catch him tomorrow in Cavaillon, then Pertuis. He was playing the whole region and they could not afford to have the signs printed so she lettered them herself. They had lost thirty in Apt. Children take the boa constrictor or the cobra home, or they paint on a moustache or simply tear it off. You cannot imagine—she shook her red head—how much vandalism there is now in France. That's why she needed to take back the sign; they had few enough for the morning; he likes his signs perfect, she said. A smudge or torn corner or line out of place, and she had to start over again.

Tonight, the stage is bright, the hall dark. Marcel Raynaud wears chinos and a checked shirt. He has scant hair and glasses and a falsely soft speaking voice, as if addressing children whom he fears to frighten; his singing voice is loud. I count eighteen other people on the stage. At the opposite end, also with a microphone, stands a younger man with chinos, checked shirt, and guitar; he does not sing as loudly but he plays with fervor. The children of the chorus seem in shock. They rock with folded arms and eyes rolled back and sing in unison when Raynaud nods. Elena whispers, "There's no harmony." She's right, of course, and it is surprising that a chorus of such size should sing just one melodic line; half the children up there seem not to sing at all. They wipe their faces furtively and shift their weight and stare out at their parents and make as little noise as possible while Raynaud warbles and shouts.

These are his compositions. They are lyrics about le Petit Prince and Simone Weil. Simone Weil, he explains, was a Jew who found God, just like Abraham before her and many others since. She was of uncertain health. She said humanity and God are like two lovers with a rendezvous who have forgotten the place. He has written a song about the place, the bridge where God and humanity meet. *"Sur le pont,"* he sings, and his acolytes sing, *"Sur le pont, pom pom."* The boy immediately to his left wears a yellow shirt and keeps his arms behind his back and sways against the beat; he keeps his eyes raised to the roof. "Can we go now?" asks Andrea.

"Not quite yet," Elena says.

"I'm hungry. I'm starving."

"Ice cream can wait," Cesca says.

"But he's no good. *Pom, pom.*" She mimes him uncannily.

"One more song," I say. We settle back. This last one deals with brotherhood and how all men are brothers, even sisters can be brothers, even parents can be friends. It takes some time. There are many choruses, and the children of the chorus sing with real fervor by now. Clearly, this number is one they can manage, and they clap in rhythm. The audience does too. A couple to my left—both blond and with a cocker spaniel on a leash who looks astonishingly like the husband—shout *"Bis, Bis!"* when it's done. Someone has left a shutter unfastened; it slams in the high wind. If we're going for ice cream and coffee, I say, now's the time to go.

VI

❊

1970–71

It was to be five years till I returned. Elena and I were married in Vermont on September 12, 1970. Two days after the wedding, our honeymoon proper began. With bounty accrued from the sale of one of my books to the movies, we planned to stay in France for six months, to travel for a year. Once more I collected a car at a factory—this time in Göteborg, a Volvo P-1800—and drove south. We lazed through Sweden, Denmark, Germany, Holland, Belgium, then France; we fetched up, two weeks later, in Châteauneuf-de-Grasse.

I had written to the Levasseurs, advising them that *les jeunes mariés* (no longer *les jeunes gens*) would be grateful if they found us something to rent. It scarcely felt appropriate to stay in the small guesthouse of Les Neiges d'Antan. We planned to live in the region but not underneath that particular roof. So they found a house in the village, and Alexander paid a visit and more or less approved.

It was a narrow, three-story structure, he wrote, at the edge of Châteauneuf-de-Grasse. Its rear garden overlooked the valley, and the place was clean—meticulous, in fact. If we wanted neighbors, we could no doubt manage there. I put his less-than-full endorsement down to pique; we were abandoning *his* handiwork, the house he had de-

signed. Mme. Rosenthal sent her congratulations and re-
gards. She too regretted we could not be immediate neighbors. We would be welcome for tea. We sent a month's
deposit. Felicity (her hairdresser would be our landlady)
took possession of the key.

We arrived in midafternoon. There is a constancy in
change; the gardens of Les Neiges d'Antan were tended
and resplendent. I could have driven the ascending switchbacks of the driveway with my eyes closed, in third gear.
The little house stood empty, untenanted since August.
Chrysanthemums bloomed by the door. The Levasseurs
were waiting; they embraced me, then Elena. Lilo Rosenthal appeared. We made our introductions—toasted our
reunion, marriage, meeting—collected the key and drove
off. Felicity acted as guide.

Châteauneuf-de-Grasse sits a quarter of a mile beneath the major artery from Nice through Vence to Grasse.
Traffic hurtles past. There is a *mairie* and a post office, a
church with a bell tower, a cluster of supply shops and local
services. The road to Grasse is lined with perfume and
postcard outlets, camera stalls, gas stations, restaurants, and
vendors of *antiquités;* the tourist trade therefore bypasses
Châteauneuf. A wall surrounds the village, and the view is
limited—not breathtaking, as from Gourdon, or domestically picturesque, as from Saint-Paul-de-Vence. Women
draw their water or hang laundry in the square beside the
boulangerie, not because they have no water in their houses,
but for the chance of a chat. Dogs sun themselves on the hot
paving or take shelter under arches. Cats have made the
rooftops their dominion, and the windows, and the alleys
that link streets.

Our street was cobbled and steep. A single small car parked in it would render passage difficult, a truck impossible. We parked beside a gate. With Felicity leading, we found our new house—the front-facing shutters closed—and she let us in. *"Ce n'est pas comme d'autrefois,"* she said, *"mais convenable quand même.* It isn't what you're used to, but it's comfortable, *non?"*

"It's comfortable, yes," I said. We carried in our bags.

"Oh darling," said Elena. "Help."

"She likes it?" Felicity asked.

The house was stuffed with bric-a-brac, a nightmare of olive-wood carvings of birds and hanging plastic ornaments and alcoves clogged with Christmas trees in styrofoam and, everywhere, black metal owls. It was airless, lightless, claustrophobic, painted hot pink and lime green. The upholstery was plastic, with clear protective sheets. The ceiling fixtures were fluorescent, the bedspread a bright tapestry of cows.

Our landlady appeared. She wore her hair in spit curls; she was stout and officious and fierce. She showed us how to work the oven, where the sheets were stored. She explained the telephone. She had an inventory of pots and flatware and towels; she demonstrated, by turning it on, that the radio turned on. She cranked the window open and clucked at a white cat outside; there was a stunted fig tree in the garden and a beach chair and a parasol stand. She said, "Everything's in order"—not making it a question—and we nodded, yes. Felicity decided that she would take advantage of the weather to promenade a little and meet Guillaume at Pré du Lac; we mustn't concern ourselves on her behalf, we must make ourselves at home. She kissed me on the cheek and was enchanted with Elena, and the two ladies left.

"It's awful," said Elena.

"Yes."

"It's not what we wanted at all."

"No."

"It's not so bad," she said. "Maybe we can manage."

I had never seen flamingos in such quantity or eight aquatints of churches in a bathroom. We opened a bottle of wine. It was October 1. We had contracted to stay for six months in a house where it would prove difficult to sleep, impossible to work. Elena, with resolute good humor, gathered the gimcrackery together and piled it in a closet; it filled the narrow shelves. We took the hanging camels down, the olive-wood donkeys and the flock of metal owls. We turned the faces of the saints around and stacked them in ranked rows. We put the doilies in drawers.

The next day dawned wetly; we moped through the dank streets. I missed the meadow full of wildflowers, the cheerful hiss of *la chaudière,* the horizon with its smudge of sea. "The French are a nation of shopkeepers," I found myself repeating; we talked of northern Italy, of Greece. There is a certain pinched, penurious aspect to life in such a rented house; the walls looked no better when bare. The lack of ornamentation at Les Neiges conveyed a kind of purity; what surrounded us in Châteauneuf were lime-green enclosures with hooks.

We visited the Levasseurs, then Lilo Rosenthal. She said again it was a shame the cottage should stand vacant. She herself was leaving for New York.

Elena tapped her foot. She lit a cigarette. She said, "With your permission, I've just grown allergic to cats."

"What?"

"My doctor tells me I'm allergic. I shouldn't stay in the village, there must have been cats in that house. I'd have hives all winter."

"You mean it?" Lily asked.

"It's terrible. I wheezed all night. I had an allergic attack."

Her skin was clear, unblemished. "Do you suppose that settles it?" I asked.

"It does. It settles it."

"It settles what?" asked Lily.

"The reason why we have to move." Elena put her hand on mine. "And why we take you up, madame, on your kind offer of protection in this medical emergency."

"*A la tienne,*" I said. "To your increasing health."

Therefore we moved into the little house and settled down. Elena kept a daybook for the trip, and her journal entry for October 3 reads, simply, "Evening, home." In some sense I date the start of our marriage from that first night in Les Neiges d'Antan; it became our shared familiar haven, not a haunted house.

We explained our situation to the Levasseurs. We

hoped we would not discommode them or make the hairdresser fierce; we would derange their privacy this winter
and hoped they might not mind. They were ravished, they
assured us, they had been hoping we'd stay. They had
bought a television lately, but the winter nights could nonetheless seem long. While we finished up in Châteauneuf,
they would do the necessary for *la petite maison.*

Like prisoners released, we packed. We did pretend
to allergies; we spoke of doctor's orders and the chagrin of
the cats. Having made excuses to an irate landlady, we left
her another month's rent. We spent an anxious hour trying
to replace the icons on the walls; we hung owls where
flamingos had flourished, attempting to remember which
coverlet had graced what chair, which church dominated
what alcove, and where the Christmas tree faced. We rearranged the cows. By the time we reached Les Neiges again,
we were giddy with relief.

The great shared sorrow of the Levasseurs was that they had
no child. Perhaps Felicity's tuberculosis had rendered her
infertile; perhaps Guillaume's slight stature made him not
wholly a man. I offer these explanations not because they
seem medically plausible, but because they troubled the
Levasseurs themselves. They lavished attention on nieces
and nephews with compensatory excess, and then they acquired a dog.

They called it Yucca; it was small and black and
vivacious and spoiled. It cavorted at Felicity's heels when

she hung out the laundry, whistling; it followed Guillaume around the gardens and teetered on the rim of the *bassin.* Mme. Rosenthal had not been happy at the prospect, they confessed; she had insisted that Yucca be spayed. They wiped her paws in the kitchen. They fashioned a bed out of cushions and wicker and bought choice morsels from the butcher and buttoned a red sweater around her in the cold. They had been prepared to change employers if Yucca could not stay.

At night we sometimes joined them on the third floor of Les Neiges. Their apartment was two rooms. The television flickered at us, indistinct; they would watch game shows and news. Felicity was knitting, Guillaume engaged in a repair—fine-fingered and attentive, frowning. They offered chocolates and nuts and honey-coated fruit. We taught one another card games and discussed the next day's schedule, who would run which errand. They might be going into Grasse, or to the cooperative for wine; they might have the black ledger open, and have been doing accounts.

Guillaume conserved string. He tied old bits together and fastened the mimosa or vines against the wind. When he needed wire to support a branch, he sheathed the branch with rubber so that it would not chafe. He cut posts every year, according to the height of the trees, and replaced them accordingly. I suggested that, instead of cutting posts to the height of one meter, then two meters, then three, he cut only to the height of three meters and save himself the bother of replacing posts. "In principle," he said, "you are correct. But in practice I dislike it. I dislike to see the post above the flower."

Lilo Rosenthal did leave for New York in October, and therefore we two couples shared the *propriété*. The mailman came at two o'clock on his loud motorcycle; trucks delivered coal. On Thursday morning the fish van arrived. It was a peaceful time. Elena's daybook for the first week of December 1970 describes the following: Monday: Day at home; Tuesday: Day at home—olive picking; Wednesday: Morning—pick olives; Thursday: Olive picking, go to olive mill; Friday: Day at home, dinner with Alex Bechstein; Saturday: Day at home, evening home with Alex; Sunday: Day at home.

There were busy times also, of course, and visitors and trips. That fall we traveled for some weeks in Germany and Austria; later we went briefly to Italy by car. There were parties to go to and give. But when I think of the season in France, I think of it as an extended pastoral—the jasmine and mimosa, the bittersweet and daisy garlands on the Christmas spruce.

We took honey from the apiaries just above Gourdon. We gathered our own olives, both for the pressing and olives in brine; a work crew from Calabria harvested the crop. Guillaume supervised them closely throughout the *récolte;* he did not trust Italians, he told me, but they were better than Algerians and he had had to choose. We watched them in the groves. A dead bird had been strapped upright to frighten the scavenging flock; children beat the topmost branches expertly with sticks. The women spread blankets beneath; they worked for a percentage of the oil.

Guillaume had invented a sifter for olives. He built a six-foot slatted ramp, with spaces large enough for the olives to fall through but small enough to catch the leaves. After a day in the field, the Levasseurs upended sacks full of olives on the ramp, and the twigs and leaves would stick. Then we could commence to sort in earnest, and the four of us could sort five hundred kilos in a week. The swallow swarms came in December, and Guillaume would break off work with regularity, rushing to the *oliviers* to fire his shotgun at the sky, rarely hitting birds.

No matter what the weather or the pleasure of the work, Felicity called a halt. At four o'clock they shared an *infusion* and fruit. She firmly believed in the effects of an *infusion* and reminded him of his tendency to chill and that even the sciatica of her pharmacist brother-in-law appeared to have been helped by tea. Sometimes he would insist on taking his tea in the fields, and then she would bring it to him on a tray with flowers, and he would sit with her, a little apart from the workers, feeling spoiled and pleased.

We spent a good deal of time with the Levasseurs that autumn and, as the winter wore on, grew familiar with their neighbors. Some of that familiarity, of course, was spurious—mere politeness on their part. But some of it, I like to think, was earned. I helped Guillaume with labor when he needed extra hands; I did the heavy lifting since his back was bad. We were made welcome as newlyweds in an openhanded fashion having something to do with our rings. We were invited to parties, card games, and afternoon *pétanques*.

Too, it was my second sojourn in the region; I was not entirely a stranger. And so the women in the

Superette—the village of Opio boasted one now—greeted us as if we were longstanding customers. We walked to market in good weather, with a string bag and used bottles to return. Madame the postmistress, monsieur the butcher, the family that ran the bakery, the candlestick maker, and men at the mill—all treated us as if we had grown privy to the place.

Shepherds brought the sheep down from their autumn pasture, then returned to the high ground in spring. We listened to the guttural complaint of goats, the trickling overflow from *le bassin,* horses in the road, the rasp of the whetstone on scythes. There was the smell of wood smoke, always, and the acrid whiff of *le grand trou* and furrows plowed by hand. I woke before first light and was at my table by six. A deck of cards lay shuffled beside the typewriter; to keep myself from fidgeting I would play solitaire. Some mornings I played fifty hands. Again the ritual of *la chaudière,* coffee and a biscuit, and the dawn bleeding out over Cannes; the cypress trees at driveway's crest would bend like strung bows in the wind. When the mistral came it came for days, and Guillaume would have a headache; he called it "mistral head." The hills of Corsica, perhaps, might be briefly visible; roosters chorused, contrapuntal, farm to farm.

We visited the regional museums: the Musée Fragonard in the center of Grasse, with its collection of furniture and clothing but few if any authentic Fragonards. He had gone north when young. The *Michelin* puts it concisely: "the demon of drawing possessed the young man, who soon left for Paris." Those artists who contrarily left Paris for the south were represented in Saint-Paul, at the Fondation Maeght. We wandered through the gardens there and spent hours also in Biot, Vence, Vallauris. We visited the War and Peace Chapel in Vallauris, the chapel in Villefranche decorated by Cocteau, the votive offerings in La Garoupe on Cap d'Antibes. The folk art of the region sits adjacent to the signed.

Still, the roster of great artists who found at least a temporary haven on the Riviera is worth pondering. Bonnard, Braque, Chagall, Dufy, Giacometti, Léger, Matisse, Miró, and Picasso—to list a few—found the light congenial. In Provence proper, of course, Cezanne and van Gogh, among others, made the landscape vivid by making it over in oil.

One can offer explanations, and art historians do. Lascaux is not far distant, and Moissac feels proximate also—when charted on a comprehensive, if not global, scale. I know no part of the world in which the visual record has been so continually, fruitfully maintained. Man has painted in the region since he began to paint. If there is something in the air of Vienna that renders its citizens musical, something in the drink of Dublin that confers agility in speech upon its populace, then surely there is something in the light of France.

Further, the living is easy—by comparison at least with the chill north. These are generalities and shot through with exceptions; others went to Brittany or Normandy instead. But the impulse to go south, to work where the lodging is cheap and wine flows readily at night, to stray among the oleanders and Aleppo pines, to watch the fishermen and farmers, *rascasses* and sea urchins and oysters, the fish heads and the one-eyed cats, the awnings on cafés and bright bead curtains clicking in the door of the *tabac:* that impulse seems, predictably, widespread. In the nineteenth century the call of the south was a clarion call, its lure a siren song. They thought of Provence as the tropics, or possibly Japan.

Add to this the temptation of good company, and you have the semblance of a colony or group. A painter goes where painters went; a voyager when possible will stop to visit friends. Cézanne came from the region, but the majority of his confreres traveled there to work. I don't mean to describe this as mere herd instinct; some artists are true solitaries and some (witness Gauguin's brief sojourn) do not remain. But the knowledge that Matisse lived nearby would surely have been welcome to Chagall or Braque, just as the knowledge that Hemingway or Stein went south might have served as an endorsement to Fitzgerald or Dos Passos or MacLeish. Signac, Bonnard, Soutine, Modigliani, and the rest, when drinking in Saint-Paul, engendered what is now the restaurant and tourist mecca of La Colombe d'Or.

To return to the trope about musical air, or tongues touched by blarney in half pints of stout, there is a magic of the southern light as difficult to specify as to ignore. A clarity, a definition that feels vivid but not harsh—a palette rendered brightly, using ochres, viridian, aquamarine. One cannot see hill villages, with their interlocking plates of rock, without seeing in them Cézanne. Or a cypress tree or sunflowers or a cane chair and cushion without van Gogh, who becomes a clear-eyed witness when you look at what he drew. What may seem excessive or mannerist in the controlled light of a gallery grows accurate outside. They were painting what consumed them or they in turn consumed: the colors of a garden, lemons, apples, bottles, oranges, and sky . . .

We saw Alex Bechstein often. He had fallen in love, he announced. It was catastrophic, absolute; he was miserably happy, and his lover would get a divorce. She was a Swiss housewife, and she lived in Berne. We would meet her, he promised, as soon as she came. He was readying his house for her, he had never been so lucky in his life. He drove down from Paris each week.

We sampled local restaurants in Plascassier, Le Collet, and Valbonne. The Opio baker still baked "the old way"—in a wood stove he stoked every morning at four. The *boules* emerged fragrant with smoke. After a month or so of unregenerate gorging we went on a diet, one of those faddish and guaranteed systems where you eat only eggs, cantaloupe, and roughage; you drink quarts of water at each meal. It seemed to work. We hated the prospect of food. At week's end, when Alex arrived, we rewarded ourselves with a meal.

He took us to a restaurant in Grasse. He was greeted, as everywhere, with fond elation; the chef and his wife were old friends. Elena looked pale. Alex lit a cigarette and ordered his mineral water; we had wine. After the first glass and an *assiette de crudités,* I began to feel human again. Elena, however, felt worse.

"I'm going to be sick," she said.

"Nonsense," Alex told her. "You'll be perfect in a minute."

"I don't think so."

"You will," he assured her. She fell to the floor.

It did not prove serious. She recovered in the air. "That's called a crash diet," she joked. We left with the proprietor persuading everyone that the young lady had not touched his food, but that it was a crisis of the liver. He himself was irreproachable, his food was in no way at fault. He had known it the minute we walked in the room, you can tell the liver's crisis by the eyes.

We began to meet "society" in and around our village. The Alpes-Maritimes is a polyglot region, traditionally subject to invaders and the influence of trade. But the Roman legions wreaked less havoc, I am sure, than do tourist charters now; they entrenched themselves less solidly than have property owners today. A morning's trip to Opio can sound like a cacophony and exercise in tongues; those who do the shopping speak in several sorts of English, German, Spanish, Polish, Dutch. The irrelevant language, it sometimes seems, is French itself.

I do not want to cluck at this or murmur disapprovingly about the way things spoil. If foreigners were not made welcome in the south, I would not have sojourned there—nor would Alexander Bechstein, for example, or Lilo Rosenthal. It is graceless at best to complain that the ark has grown crowded with beasts, that they ought to be more chary at the gate.

Dirk Bogarde lived behind Les Neiges, Julia Child on the opposite hill. At a cocktail party in Saint-Cézaire, we met Peter Wilson, the chairman of Sotheby's, Sybille Bedford, and a host of ensconced expatriates—Englishmen there for the sake of their budgets or privacy or health.

A Polish count of questionable credentials and considerable taste (attested to by framed photographs) in racehorses and women rented the villa above us; he left without settling his bills. Italians in Ferraris paid for their houses in cash. Mystery writers and movie stars cavorted near Valbonne. Old royalty and industrialists and artists like Charles Aznavour, Pablo Picasso, and Somerset Maugham lived behind locked gates. Years later, when Baby Doc Duvalier was at last expelled from Haiti, he moved to safe quarters in Grasse.

The mayor of Grasse in Napoleon's time had just such a problem to solve. When the emperor returned from Elba, on March 1, 1815, he landed at Golfe-Juan. The route Napoléon today—from Golfe-Juan to Grenoble via Saint-Vallier, Castellane, Digne, and Sisteron—attests to his hard progress north. The citizens were less than certain which attitude to choose—whether to welcome the conquering hero or shun the renegade. In light of his fortunes thereafter, they would be punished or praised. The Hundred Days were starting and the verdict not yet in. So, according to the story, the mayor of Grasse made an evenhanded compromise: he did not permit Bonaparte inside the town but provisioned him amply outside. They picnicked in the fields.

Elena tried to learn to bake the local *boules*. The baker was suspicious. Why should the elegant lady waste hours on a loaf when she could buy the proper thing for a few francs? Was she intending a business, was she worried that his methods were impure? We assured him of our admiration, our despondency at not being able to eat his bread daily, our desire to retain the taste of Opio when far away. We would, *hélas,* be unable to patronize his bakery next autumn, and would be honored if he helped us imitate his inimitable product, to allay the sorrow of departure.

He showed her how to shape the dough and how to let it rise. The secret was the flour and the yeast. We bought local flour and yeast. Julia Child and Simone Beck, we learned, had certain ingredients flown from Manhattan to Nice; otherwise their recipes would fail. They wrote for an American audience, and "mastering the art of French cooking" entails therefore a kind of translation. The butter and the flour in America have different consistencies; the yeast is not the same. Elena is a splendid baker, but she failed. Daily the *boules* were too thick or too dry; they did not rise or did not develop a crust. After twenty tries, she gave it up; you cannot prepare for or transport a *madeleine* . . .

The foreign legion has its own sort of solidarity; many of the more permanent strangers made us welcome in the south. Of those we came to know, I want to mention three. The first is Genevieve Mills. Her husband, Ted, was an expatriate American; she had made a career of her wacky foreign ways as an expatriate Frenchwoman on "The Jack Paar Program." She had withdrawn from show business but still had a theatricality about her, an entertainer's flair. She was a chantoosy and a floozy on TV, but thoroughly grounded in life.

They lived in a fine house on the outskirts of Saint-Paul-de-Vence. Her father, a *vieux colon,* was deciding if he would remain in Paris or settle with his daughter; he was frail and white-haired and ramrod-straight and he despised de Gaulle. He had built the railroad to Kinshasa, and he could not understand why Frenchmen should not ride that train in peace.

Genevieve managed her household with an offhand grace. She cooked with flourish and skill. She was passionate about her flowers and her dogs and furniture and books. She had made a reputation out of mispronouncing English, she assured us; she'd been Mademoiselle Malaprop. You can say the most outrageous things as long as you inflect them and don't seem to know what you say. And so she found us charming; we shouldn't worry that our French was less than letter-perfect; she herself preferred it to French spoken with a German accent, or a British, or a Dutch. She gave us *moules farcies* and elaborate quenelles and endorsed the life we planned to live. She found it romantic, she told us, and unrealistic and pure.

Less realistic and more pure was an eighty-year-old painter named Ernestina Haas. She came from the same consequential Viennese society as Lilo Rosenthal and had known Lilo since childhood. The four of us had lunch. She was tall and thin and powerful, with the face of a Roman senator—close-cropped white hair, a prominent nose, deep-set eyes. She was somehow related to Freud. When young she had married a doctor, had gone with him to Borneo, and spent years in the Far East. She was invested with what I can only call a savage impatience, a sense of immediacy: she ate with her hands, not utensils; she smoked cigars and swore. That which might have seemed pretentious in a twenty-year-old hoyden seemed, in this old woman, authenticity itself.

Later, we would come to know her well. She lived in a large open house near Bargemon, in the wilder reaches of the Var. Her rooms were sparsely furnished, her possessions bright. She had a mask or two and woven wall hangings and baskets of dried herbs. She lived alone, though rumor had it that, since her fifties, she had abjured the company of men and elected that of women. Aged and ill and absent-minded as she had become, she had nonetheless a truly commanding presence, an electric sexuality; her paintings could render a landscape erotic, her watercolors of fruit and her trees were nudes.

Somewhere in New Guinea, she would tell us proudly, she left convention behind. She described the widespread cannibalism in Borneo, and when I asked if she had partaken in the village feasts, she answered yes, of course. I asked her, half-joking, what part of the body was best. She raised her hand and bit the flesh at the base of her thumb. She licked her lips.

Some of her ferocity was pretense, possibly. Her talent was finite, her isolation acute. When she, this outsize woman wearing black, folded herself to the seat of the car, it was as though a buzzard settled on a branch. Yet she represented—represents to me still, though she died long ago—a way of being in the world, a flouting of the commonplace, a single-minded artistry whose public recognition had been small. Ernestina did not mind. She did not complain, in any case; she stayed the course. She would rather have this shard, she told me—holding up a piece of painted clay—than the Limoges and Meissen of her youth.

The third of the trio, James Baldwin, was famous. If Genevieve had been a television personality who elected private life and Ernestina Haas had painted in obscurity, then Baldwin was a public man whose stay in France could be construed as a self-conscious exile: the black artist in retreat. It had been so proclaimed by him, and critics would treat it as such. Our real and growing friendship belongs to another chapter and visit, but it began in the winter of 1971. He lived not far from Genevieve Mills, on the outskirts of Saint-Paul.

I had met him the previous winter, in Istanbul. I was working on the screenplay for the film of my first novel, and the director knew Baldwin, and Baldwin was in town. We had a drink together and went to *Fortune and Men's Eyes,* a play he directed in Turkish. Not knowing Turkish, I was less than enthralled, and the meeting did not matter much and the evening was a blur. Then I ran into Jimmy in Cannes. We were standing on line at the American Express office, and the wait was tedious. While I readied myself to do battle, again, with that travel agent who had sent me to Le Havre and a nonexistent ferry, I recognized Baldwin behind me. We shook hands. We exchanged politenesses, and I said that the director who had introduced us would be passing through with his new wife, and maybe we could get together for a meal or drink.

I was surprised, I think, at his alacrity; we went to his house the next day. And the daybook for our final ten days in Provence lists five such occasions: dinner at his house, at ours, at a restaurant in Saint-Paul-de-Vence, and many talks and walks. He was completing *No Name in the Street;* he planned to remain in France and would do so for years. His openhanded welcome, his insistence that we call as soon as we came back meant much, as did his cheerful certainty that we would return.

Our marriage that had started in a whirlwind of hotels had come to settle down in the most benign of privacies. When I look at the daybook again (November 1: Day at home, drinks with Ted and Genevieve Mills, dinner at Les Oliviers in Saint-Paul-de-Vence; November 2: Quiet day at home; November 3: Day at home, Grasse—shopping; November 4: Quiet day at home, trip to Vallauris for Christmas gifts") I am grateful for the silence there, the slow accumulation and comfort-rounds of routine. Elena and I began to know each other in the little house. Life seems far busier now; the getting and spending increase. When at the end of a month we wonder together how it hurtled past, we speak of that stay at Les Neiges: the soft sift of time through the glass.

We left. We undertook our trip in earnest and went around the world. We drove, via Paris and Boulogne, to London. We visited my family and arranged for visas; this took weeks. We flew to Istanbul. Then we made our way through countries it is no longer simple to visit: Iran, Afghanistan. That traveler who's seen the Himalayas and the Hindu Kush saw them on this trip. We journeyed to Nepal and the Ceylon that had just become Sri Lanka; we had a first exposure to India and Thailand, Malaysia, Indonesia, China, and Japan.

There are, it scarcely needs repeating, many wonders in this world. The beaches of Bali make those that line the Côte d'Azur look ugly and corrupt; Kabul and Katmandu are far stranger than Cannes. One eats as well in Hong Kong or Singapore as at La Bonne Auberge; the art of Bangkok, Bombay, and Kyoto easily surpasses what is on view at Antibes. The garlic that Ford Madox Ford called the hallmark of civilization can be found in markets other than those of Provence.

But such comparisons are pointless or beside the point. What happened elsewhere happened elsewhere and is not now germane. When we landed in America and began our actual married life, it would be of Les Neiges we spoke most fondly and most often—the small house with hearts on the shutters, and the climbing roses, and the fig tree by the door. We would return, we promised each other, as soon as possible. It had been our first home.

VII

1987

"It's boring."

"What is?"

"*A Tale of Two Cities.* Charles Dickens is a *re*tard, Dad."

"He's not. He's a great writer."

"Right."

"When I was your age I read *A Tale of Two Cities.* I loved it. And *Great Expectations.*"

"Right."

"*David Copperfield. Oliver Twist.*"

"I liked the one with Scrooge. Maybe some of those others are worth it. But this is *boring.*"

"It can't be, Cesca. You've got the wrong Dickens. 'The best of times, the worst of times.'"

"See what I mean? A retard. He can't even make up his mind."

"It's a figure of speech, a reversal. Things can be their own opposite."

"Well, this is its own opposite. A famous book that's bad."

"You have to read it, anyhow. For school."

"Alack and welladay," she says. "Ay me. Begone. Oh woe."

We have settled in by now, and I keep a notebook. It is not so much a journal as a set of work-points, a series of jottings out here on the porch. The sun is high by eight. I water the few flowers while it still is shady, then sit beneath the trellis in the increasing heat. The notebook is leather, dark red.

July 7. France has, approximately, five times the land mass of England and the same population—therefore this comparative amplitude of space. (Water dripping from the cistern; the loud cicadas; men asleep on benches or under cypress trees. The *marronniers* immense . . .) The road signs are less clear than I remembered, the men on the *motos* less jolly. At each crossroads one is instructed, though the instructions make scant sense. Still, it's a nation that likes clarity in road and sign; it is not accidental that their deconstructionists now reign supreme or that they spawned semiotics.

The English took their road markers down so that the Germans' threatened invasion would bring them nowhere clear. The French were too proud of directional markings, too sure of the Maginot line. Perhaps these are the leavings of the Roman roads, those straight spokes thrusting out from the hub. And the trees were planted, so tradition has it, by Napoleon's armies in order that the future's soldiery might enjoy shade where they march.

Cherries and melons and peaches for sale in the roadside stalls, the melons from Cavaillon small, thick-fleshed, and tart . . . Ants marshaling on a mulberry leaf or in the sugar bowl . . . The long coomb of the Lubéron traversed every morning by jets . . . The long lean blonde with her gentleman at the pool of the Hôtel de Guilles, breasts sunning when she lies beside him, tying her suit up to swim.

I have not seen a wooden house in Lourmarin, or one with expanses of glass. In even the most modish village, new houses are built "in the old way," using concrete instead of stone, but with the same stucco finish and little windows to keep out the light . . . The Lyonnais industrialist who wants to build a hotel here, since his wife prefers this village to Lyons; she has an insincere engaging smile and excellent legs and a black nursemaid for her son; they sit in an open Jeep, surveying the site, the radio on . . . A scorpion, this morning, by the sink in the garage. An increasing sense of the rigor of this climate, its harsh clarity. Nothing tropical or lush about these fields . . .

The holding tanks for the Cave Cooperative are the size of silos. The *patron* enters laughing, hoisting his cup of *vin blanc mousseux,* wiping his mouth with his sleeve . . . This earth as red as Georgia's, and the ochre pits in Roussillon as gaudy as the painted desert; the lavender like Indian paintbrush, the hillsides here like those of Cape Cod, pine and scrub oak and weed . . . This insistent habit of comparison, the wanderer's coordinates: formulations that bespeak familiarity, so that we feel at home.

July 8. The difference, for the traveler, between arrival and return is crucial. The thrill of recognition doubles that of cognition itself; "to come back" is not "to go." But I read some years ago of a couple from the Midwest who had been married in Manhattan fifty years before. For their anniversary, these "golden codgers" chose to relive their honeymoon; they had not visited New York in all the time between. They stayed, again, at the Plaza Hotel. Although it had become much more expensive and less clean, they ate at the Oak Room the meal they had eaten when young. Hand-in-hand they then walked from the Plaza, passing the fountain, nodding at the horse-drawn carriages, reconstructing their first moonlit stroll through Central Park. A policeman stopped them, saying, "Are you crazy? It's not safe." They were not dissuaded. They explained their purpose to him, and he said, "Go ahead." Then he walked fifty paces behind, swinging his nightstick, providing the margin of safety while they ambled together in front, oblivious, admiring June's moon.

"I must hurry off this letter for I feel some more abstractions coming on and if I did not quickly fill up my paper I would again set to drawing and you would not have your letter." So writes van Gogh, in English, to John Russell in June 1888, from Arles. "Am working at a Sower: the great field *all violet* the sky & sun very yellow. It is a hard subject to treat."

July 9. Andrea is a fiery child, mobile in feature, decisive of mood. She emulates her sister, then wants to murder her, then mourns the anticipated future when we will be dead. She is tender-hearted, flinty-eyed—with a single dimple in her cheek. She was born with a dislocated hip and spent much of her first two years in a body brace, then a cast. Released, she has rocketed everywhere.

We rehearse the words she knows in French and count them daily, accumulating. She knows how to count to one hundred, and, in consequence, one hundred words. She knows some words for color—red, yellow, green, purple, brown. She can say swimming pool and bread and garbage and green beans and ice cream and dog. She translates bathing suit and cat and please and good night and thank you and good morning and chocolate-filled croissant; she can ask the time and for Orangina and coffee and salt; she can say shut up.

Cesca, thirteen, likes the language and has studied it for three years. She has a poster of the Eiffel Tower in her bedroom and one of Notre Dame. She reads *Elle* magazine with avid interest and dreams of French clothes and perfume. When I was her age I remember sitting in a restaurant in Paris, asking for ice in the water. I asked repeatedly and did so at my mother's prompting. The waiter nodded, raised an eyebrow, and withdrew. He returned with strawberry sherbet and set it by my plate. I said I had asked for water—very cold, with ice—and he said, yes, *fraise glacée.* I had mumbled the word for water but repeated that I wanted it cold, *frais,* and then said ice, not ice cubes, *glace,* not *glaçons.* This delighted my parents; it was a family joke. I remember that waiter with horror—his slicked-down hair, his smirk, smug rectitude, the buttons on his jacket and thin line of powder at his collar, the fact that my father nonetheless left him a tip.

So we watch Francesca order green beans and get green beans, water and get water. We let her make selections at the bakery, the pharmacy, the postcard rack. Her French improves. Yet her language is the language of all tourists, that of commerce, weather, food. I have wondered, often, about the language-set of boys and girls in the commercial streets, how they modulate so smoothly from English to German to French. They speak a smattering of Italian, Arabic, some Spanish; they describe the glories of a carpet or a leather coat in six or seven tongues. They have the terminology of bargaining and also the language of praise—the beauty of texture or color, value in terms of investment. They can seem persuasive, even fluent in their discourse; they are brilliant linguists who choose a life in trade.

And this is partly true. It is also the case, of course, that they may be illiterate, bereft of education, competent in what is serviceable only to the service they perform. Ask about a matter not related to the purchase, and you'll get a gaze as blank as that which greets the desert traveler who describes varieties of rain. The word for *ice* means little in the Sudan, I imagine, nor would *strawberry* bulk large in the

Inuit vocabulary. Usage is all. When we joined the olive harvest I learned many words for olive, wind, and frost. So the context of these pages determines the content thereof. I will not write about—though they matter to me very much—those who did not matter to me in the south of France.

Such a process of exclusion is characteristic, perhaps, of the stages of age. We make new friends while losing old; we cannot focus on first love while living with a second; we change our eating, sleeping, drinking habits over time. It is enlargement and contraction, the systole and diastole of the breathing animal, the very rhythm of replenishment: we die daily, living, and come closer to completion with each line. The spectacle of those who try to stave off change—old men with parlor suntans and toupees, old women with face-lifts and stiletto heels—looks no less disconcerting than does the reverse: an adolescent trading stock-options in a three-piece suit. The shellfish shucks its shell, enlarging, as the snake its skin.

But, unlike the tree or horseshoe crab, we shrink who grow. At a certain stage our appetites diminish, and we call them therefore refined. The system of cuisine perfected by French cooks is organized by waste, reduction, the re-finer's fire. If you have a hunting party and scant refrigera-tion, you face the problem of two hundred partridge and eighty quail for dinner. This food will not be offered to the hungry multitude nor taste any good in a week. And so we have the stockpot, the process of reduction; one cup of soup fit for a king derives from eighty quail.

I do not want to exaggerate. Some systems of distri-bution make sense; some hunting parties bring back food for the whole tribe. And those who hunt and gather where supplies are less abundant must be equitable in sharing; it was the very copiousness of supply for haute cuisine that made distinction plausible, the four and twenty blackbirds stewing daintily in pie.

All this is far afield from Cesca's menu French. We eat lunch beneath the slope of Mont Ventoux. Petrarch was the first to have climbed the "windy mountain" or to have recorded the climb; he ascended, with his brother, in 1336. The view is no doubt more impressive today, since the summit has been stripped. They used the straight tall cedars for the masts of the French fleet. There is no second growth. The rock scree looks like snow. Bicyclists weave up the hill. They "engage the mountain," the restaurateur says.

Mont Ventoux rises alone. It makes a startling pyramid—visible from afar, with unimpeded vistas from its crest. From the north face you can see the Alps, from the south the Rhône Valley; the Pyrenees lie far to the southwest. A girl drinking coffee in the courtyard made me think of Petrarch's Laura—or how one might imagine her if casting for a film. Blond ringlets, a fine-featured profile, a classic equine face, smiling, demure. She was sitting with an older woman, eyes cast down. They conversed in low tones. Then she lit a cigarette and showed bad teeth and black hair in her armpits and laughed a braying laugh. As if there were a cult here of the virgin whore—Aphrodite Pandaemon.

Cesca wants snails. Andrea is horrified. *"Snails!"* We order a dozen, then trout. Andrea eats her daily allowance of biscuits, then French fries with ketchup, *pommes frites.* I want to take them to Venasque, to visit Boethius's tomb. I tell them the little I know. He translated Aristotle; he died in 524; he wrote *The Consolation of Philosophy* while in an Italian jail. My grandmother loved Boethius. She had a worn blue leather-bound German translation of his book and took it with her everywhere, tapping the binding, saying, "Such is life. It's in Boethius." I never saw her read it; she was nearly blind. But in her great old age, sunk into the semblance of meditation, she would rouse herself to stroke the book and thumb its pages yet again and say, "Boethius said it: the consolation of philosophy. Such is life. It's here."

I still can taste her *himbersaft,* the raspberry syrup she poured into water and stirred. A mountainous, decisive lady, my grandmother took us out on "nature walks," pointing her carved cane at trees and demanding to know their names. If I got it right ("Monkey tree, granny, and chestnut, and oak") I could have *himbersaft* and yogurt and chocolate in her room. Karl Schmidt-Rottluff made her jewelry. She smoked like an ill-pointed chimney, dripping ash; she wore only black or gray. Her English disappeared with time; she died at ninety-six, blind, in my uncle's London home. "Send me a postcard," she used to say. "But maybe I won't answer. In the country that I'm going to, they don't deliver mail."

The church itself lies a mile from Venasque in the flatland underneath the rise on which the town is perched. It is a working church, not monument; the fifth-century baptistry within Venasque has tour guides and music and postcards. Here in the hot meadow there are worshippers, not tourists—a white-headed man on his knees, a needle-thin widow in black. The stone has wheels and runes; it sits behind the confessional. It is, I read, an excellent example of Merovingian carving. The bishop of Venasque and Carpentras, whose service here this stone commemorates, watched Mont Ventoux from his window longer precedent to Petrarch than Petrarch is to us.

There is consolation and philosophy sufficient in arithmetic; the spelling looks wrong. This bishop was Bohetius and not Boethius; the *h* has been transposed. He is not my philosopher; we had been misinformed. The laundry on the line outside snaps and flutters in the wind; there has been *"un bon coup de mistral."*

July 12. You can tell an artist from Provence by the shadow cast. "I knew you by your shadow" is the Kalahari Bushman greeting; this small, proud people apparently exaggerate the stature of the man they meet by praising his shadow's long length. So a painter from Provence—no matter how much influenced by Flemish ways, or Frankish—will give shadow to a figure where it stands. It is the necessary consequence of light.

July 13. The Château de Lourmarin has been in part restored. There are several stages to its age. Most recently it has served as a foundation for young artists, a place they come to play the piano, write, or paint. There are samovars and Spanish tables and Piranesi prints; these attest to the eclectic collecting impulse of the industrialist who last

owned the structure, Robert Laurent-Vibert. He died in a car crash in 1925 at forty-one, a bachelor. His will endowed a foundation for young artists, and it is a success. When we take the guided tour—the guide suggesting we should admire the staircase, the beaming, the salamander incised in rock in honor of François I—a girl is practicing, loudly and badly, for a recital tomorrow. She pauses with barely suppressed impatience while we hurry past; as soon as the door to the music room closes she starts in again on the phrase. Rachmaninoff, Elena says, the second movement, she'll get it, I imagine, but she keeps getting it wrong.

July 15. Francesca watches television. She does so, she insists, in order to improve her French; she has seen these shows in America and likes to watch them dubbed. The reruns are many and various: soap operas, situation comedies, "Facts of Life" and "Three's Company" and "Hotel" and "Love Boat" and "Dynasty," police shows in the early evening, cartoons on Saturday. Tom and Jerry cackle in French, and so does Mickey Mouse. *"Arnold et Willie"* was once "Diff'rent Strokes," and there is something comical about these altered inflections, Arnold's quick black canniness transformed into argot.

But it takes us time to understand why the shows sound wrong. There is no canned applause. The French use no dubbed laughter. So everything takes a split second too long; the intervals for double takes, the programmed pauses feel empty. Cesca watches the French version of quiz shows, game shows, MTV. Andrea, whose attention span is in any case much shorter, turns away impatiently, saying "It's stupid. It's dumb."

The dubber represents, for me, one paradigm of the artist. When you notice how good a job has been done, it no longer is a good job. Like Joyce's dramatist, "invisible, refined out of existence, indifferent, paring his fingernails," the dubber most succeeds when no one sees him there. The witness who commends the excellent work of translation has registered the failure of that work instead.

"Do you miss your friends, Andrea?"

"Yes."

"Badly?"

"Not so badly. I wish we got more mail."

"You have to write to get mail back."

"Cesca gets letters. I wrote eleven postcards yesterday. I wasted all that time."

"But it takes time for the mail to arrive. They're probably writing you back."

"Anna never writes me back. She's not my friend."

"She's jealous, maybe. Maybe she's traveling too."

"I sent her my address."

"We'll be home again before you know it. Before all those letters arrive."

"If only I could call them. If only the telephone worked."

"You got a letter yesterday."

"Just one. And it's from Granny, it doesn't really count."

"It counts."

"You always get more mail. You never don't get mail."

"Bills mostly. Things to answer. I wish the mail stopped coming, sometimes. Like how peaceful it is here *without* a telephone."

"When we go shopping later, can I get myself *cracottes?*"

July 19. English writers seem to have as strong an affinity for the Midi as did Flemish painters before. A casual list of authors in this century who built or renovated or rented homes here could furnish a kind of "literary little England" for the enterprising tour guide with a degree and a bus. There are Huxley, Lawrence, Ford and Wells, Durrell, Wilson, Greene and Coward, Maugham, Bedford, Connolly—I list them at random on purpose, following neither chronology nor the alphabet. Not all of them stayed here, of course, and few are best known for their sojourns in France; some wrote travel books about a world elsewhere. (Witness *Mornings in Mexico, Reflections on a Marine Venus, Journey Without Maps.*) There is a story, possibly apocryphal, about a camel trip that Maugham took across the Sahara. He carried Proust's massive work with him and, having finished a page, tore it loose. He did not want the total weight and lightened his progress, sheet by chapter, until at the end of

the journey there was nothing left. He owned, no doubt, a second copy at home. But somewhere decomposing on five hundred miles of the Sahara lie the pages of *A la recherche du temps perdu*. This seems to me, if true, one proper version of usage—the camel track littered with language, the book in the head and not pack.

July 22. The poet John Clare required his intimate landscape so deeply—the view from the window unchanging—that he went mad when moved. What his father and grandfather had looked at delimited his sense of the permissible; what he had not seen before went beyond the pale. Or think of those weavers with eidetic memory, those who know the way a rug is woven with no recourse to design. They may pick up the pattern with no shift of rhythm, without a shape established or a picture to consult.

The innovative artist, however, being what he is, cannot be what he reports on; the scribe is set apart. Much has been written of the sorrow and the privilege of such apartness, the dizzying vistas entailed. What I mean to point to is its inescapability: how the observer alters each scene and speech observed. Elena says she's happy here, now, in the house. Hers is the gift of concentration, and the present tense. . . .

Stendhal wrote his *Mémoires d'un touriste* one hundred and fifty years ago; it remains a model of idiosyncratic response to the stimulus of travel. Mérimée, Flaubert, Daudet, the Goncourt brothers, Zola (who, like Cézanne, was born in Aix) wrote at least briefly on the region, and some of them did so at length. Lamartine, George Sand, Pichot, Canongue, Dumas—the list enlarges with the looking, and there is nothing new to write under the Provençal sun. One might compile a lexicon of referents to *sun*—as inescapable in literature as life.

We read *Little Women* aloud. Elena and I take turns, reading three chapters nightly. It has become a ritual observance, and if we know we cannot read at night we do so in the late afternoon. The tale is mawkish, overlong; it candy-coats reality and is often coy. Yet I am moved to near-tears by the plight of the family, mournful when they mourn, and happy when they celebrate. Something in the very act of reading the story aloud releases it from private censure; the speed of utterance is so much slower, more compelling, than that of silent scanning. There is a communion, nearly, in the communal audience, Linda and our daughters on the couch.

So comedy is funnier when other people laugh, and sorrow more convincing in shared silence, downcast looks. Therefore 1987 will be the summer of *Little Women,* as some summers ago in England we read Laura Ingalls Wilder, the adventures of her pioneering clan. Nor can I see *Little House on the Prairie* without a mental image of the girls' bedroom in Sandhurst-Hawkhurst, the window seat I read from in the English dark. Now Lourmarin contains New England's Concord, and Jo and Amy and Beth and the rest enlarge our company. Mr. Lawrence, that gruff benefactor, peers in through the window, hands clasped behind his back.

July 29. Two kilometers from Lourmarin, the Hôtel de Guilles offers tennis and swimming. There is a stable nearby. Some patrons are *sportif;* they arrive on bicycles or go rock-climbing at Buoux. Others loll by the pool, eating ice cream, reading the paper, daubing each other with oil. The pool is large, well tended, and the view of the Lubéron expansive: fields of lavender, then scraggling fruit trees and melons, scree, cliff. Those who stay at the hotel use the facilities freely; residents of Lourmarin can sign on daily or monthly or annually to join the Club de Guilles.

It is an inviting prospect, and July is hot. The children love to swim. I hope to make an "arrangement," therefore, with the hotel manager; several days running I go to his office. He proves difficult to find. He is on vacation. His niece cannot help me, he will return next week. Meantime, we use the pool. We bring towels from the house. We tip the waiters lavishly and buy expensive drinks. Topless women smile at us, and their escorts scowl.

One afternoon a stocky man with a white shirt, shock of brown hair, and brown moustache appears. He leans forward when he walks, as if about to break into a run. He invites me to his office, smiling; he has just returned from Venice and inquires if I speak Italian, then says I am a sympathetic type. His desk is piled with photographs, with correspondence, stacks of bills; a blackboard above it lists vacancies in the hotel for the next three months. There are few. He rummages through paper and finds a plastic folder, listing prices of the pool per person or per family, by day or week or month. His posted charges are outlandish, so much so that I cannot believe he intends them; it would cost five hundred dollars for the family per week. He has no membership forms, no receipts; he repeats that I appear to be *"un type sympa."* He wants me to bribe him. I do.

As the weeks wear on, however, the staff's good will wears thin. He is the only man I've bribed, and his subordinates keep asking for our room key or address. There are two possibilities. Either he has told them of our thousand-franc agreement, and they want to get in on the action, or he has not told them, and they want to settle up. The chain of command is complex. Those who tend the pool do not also run the café; those who serve lunch on the patio do not collect the mattresses or chairs.

We're not gate-crashers, clearly, and we smile and pay for ice cream or drinks; we speak sufficient French and drive a decent car. We have children and look married and stay longer in the region than would people passing through. The manager is courteous, respectful; they dare not throw us out. But they wonder what we're doing (the mistral strong, the water cold, the septic system reeking from the week-long continual revelry of *le quatorze juillet*) and how polite they need be.

A clarity obtains in dealing with the French. There is nothing subtle or mysterious to commerce in the south; they do not decide to trust you or take umbrage unprovoked. Rather, the system is simple. Those you tip will make you welcome in the future; those you fail to will not fail to register the lack. But it must not be excessive or you're taken for a fool. The rational man measures cost. There is direct proportion here, a perfect equivalence of service offered for services purchased: a clear-eyed incremental responsiveness to cash.

It does not seem so simple elsewhere—in America, for instance, or the Far East. I have often failed to offer what had been expected, or tried to give a tip where nothing had been sought. The last week of our stay the wind is high. Leaves and berries blow into the pool. We leave before our welcome would have had to be refinanced; the manager assures me we will be welcome back.

VIII

1973

In January of 1973, Elena and I did return. This time we flew directly to Nice and met the Levasseurs. They waited at the gate. We planned to remain through May. The Nice airport is located along the water's edge, and the Pré-Alpes rise behind it gaudily; the scenery is splendid yet on a human scale. The ride home *felt* like riding home; we recognized the road, the shortcuts, the finally complete construction at the corner in Le Collet.

Guillaume and Felicity were full of news. The weather had been foul; it had been raining all week. They were sorry Yucca stayed at home, but she would have been too active in the car. They had the most marvelous plans. They were planning a house at the edge of Les Neiges; Lilo Rosenthal had sold them—at a good price, we must understand, at something they could manage and *sans doute* as compensation, so they could remain in the region but not in the *grenier*—a building plot. They had enough space for the construction and needed to cut down no trees. We would look at the plans, we would see. They would start with the foundation as soon as the weather improved.

Our first order of business, however, was a car. This time I had bought nothing in advance. I had written Guillaume to ask him to look for *une voiture quelconque:* something to last out our visit, something to get us to market and back that we could sell when leaving. He had found it, he informed me, a "funny little car," and we shouldn't look too closely, but it ran.

I had never heard of the vehicle before: an NSU Prinz. It was off-white, dented like a bumper car at an amusement park; it had a sunroof and backseat and windshield wipers and functioning lights and a horn. It cost three thousand francs. There were additional charges and the usual thicket of French bureaucracy, so that the total purchase, at the then-current rate of exchange, was five hundred dollars. I sold it, five months later, for very nearly the same.

But "what a falling off was there"—from Alfa-Romeo to Volvo sports coupe to a fifth-hand NSU Prinz. If I chart the relation to place in terms of how to travel through it, then this was unadorned reality indeed. We came to love "the little Prince" for its very faults. It coughed and sputtered into life; it cornered like a galleon in a gale. Its tires belonged on a bicycle. Once Elena, returning from market, coming up the entrance drive, swerved too close to the side of a switchback and brushed against a rose bush by the retaining wall. Ten minutes later, the tire was flat; we extracted thorns. No other car I know of has been so affected by a rose.

It caught on fire, too. The battery was underneath the backseat—a platform, really, supported by springs. When weight depressed this bench, the metal springs made contact with the battery and, after some minutes, the cushion ignited; first came the smell, then smoke. We were horrified. We tumbled out and jumped away; I inched back heroically to dismantle the banquette, throwing groceries out helter-skelter, lifting the seat. It reeked. It had happened before; there was a charred half circle on the cushion's underside.

Guillaume was philosophical. He discussed the purchase price. He reminded me that this wasn't the Volvo, that sporty white model made famous in France by the rerun of a series called "The Saint." We jerry-rigged a shield between the battery and springs; it failed to work. When weight was on the rear seat for more than a few minutes, fire started. Then we raised the cushion, and it stopped.

Since Elena and I were most often alone, this came to be a manageable problem. Like any regular menace, its edge grew dull with time. If a third party joined us for a drive, we had only to instruct them to sit on the side away from the battery; this acted as a kind of counterweight, keeping the springs raised. We put our bags there too.

One evening, however, we drove two friends to Nice. They were taking the train; they had luggage. The car was therefore heavily weighted, and the trip not short. Without incident we reached the *gare,* embraced and sent them on their way, and started back to Grasse. It was early evening, I remember, the sky already dark, the streetlights lit. Soon enough the telltale smell, the acrid beginnings of flame arose from the rear seat. "Man your stations," said Elena. "Fire drill."

We were practiced at this, unperturbed; I pulled over to the curb. We got out unhurriedly and dismantled the banquette and waved the smoke away and waited for the odor to subside. A woman tapped Elena on the back.

She was wielding an umbrella, outraged. "You can't do this," she hissed. "You're not allowed to, here."

I started to explain about our problem with the seat, the little fire, that we would be leaving again. She pointed to the sign beside us: *Défense de Stationner.* I tried to say we were not parking, had no desire to remain; she threatened to call the police. We dressed the Prinz again in some semblance of propriety and left.

Guillaume could sound embittered; the more he came to trust me, the more he would complain. The Côte d'Azur was overrun with noisy children not his own. There was traffic and construction everywhere he went; things were not as he remembered them or as they ought to be. There had been drug troubles in Biot. He still took Felicity to the Croisette, but it was not pleasant any longer with the drugs and cars. It was pleasant in the rain, when the Americans— he smiled at me, apologetic—and therefore the photographers stayed inside. It was pleasant, sometimes, to eat in restaurants, but the standard of cooking declined and the prices rose. The butcher was not clean.

Fraternity, he told me, was men who slept with men. Equality was not a question of taxes, since the poor got poorer, and the rich stayed rich. For the sport of it, he read, drivers would run over dogs. Liberty was filth inscribed in the grottoes of Saint-Cézaire; the walls were pocked with names there, with telephone numbers to call.

And people wasted rope. People flung bottles and

paper from cars, and they had had to close schools. There were advertisements now on television, and he had heard football players were bribed. Little enough was certain in this world, but he had thought football was certain. Many things were grievous, were changing for the worse; there was no grandeur left in France, no glorious ambition since Charles de Gaulle was gone.

Les Neiges did not seem changed, however, nor did our relation to the Levasseurs. We admired their construction site, the plans; we discussed the quality of roof tile and the problem with the pitch of the garage. Alexander would have solved it, they maintained. He would have been willing, entirely helpful; he would have demonstrated how best to keep the view.

Six months before, he had died. (*"Votre père doit être désolé.* Your father must be desolated," said Guillaume.) It had been a quick but not unexpected collapse. Alex had been fighting cancer for some time; he continued to smoke, lost a lung. The cancer metastasized and went to his brain and proved inoperable. His final months were agony, a ravening gauntlet of pain. My father flew to see him and came back shaken, death-trammeled. "He couldn't speak," he said. One of Alexander's final conscious acts had been to sketch a house plan for the Levasseurs, but he had not had the leisure to iron out small details of design.

"You understand," said Guillaume. "He did it as a favor, he refused to take a sou."

"I understand," I said.

"But they did get married. She nursed him like an angel. She was splendid. *Vous verrez.*"

"We'll see?" Elena asked.

"She lives at La Lauve, in their house. Madame Bechstein. You'll meet her. You'll see."

But Madame Bechstein, Maija, was for the moment in Berne. She was "disposing her affairs" and would be back in March; we would understand, as soon as we met her, her angelic ways. If he had not died so horribly, the garage would be situated as it should have been, *comme il fallait;* they lacked him every week. Mme. Rosenthal was desolated also. Alex had the spirit of a young man even in his *troisième âge.* It was unthinkable, they said, to think of him as dead.

Jimmy Baldwin, however, remained. This time he welcomed us like long-lost friends. He had established a work-pattern and an entourage. He had a chauffeur large enough to double as a bodyguard, a cook, a companion named Philippe who acted as a kind of secretary-manager, and various others whose function is less easy to describe. There would be a dancer or painter in tow—old lovers or associates from some project in the offing, or projected, or long past. They came from Italy, America, Algeria, Tunisia, Finland. Brothers and nephews passed through.

We were rarely less than six at table, and more often ten. The cook and the *femme de ménage* came and went; the men stayed on. They treated their provider with a fond deference, as if his talent must be sheltered from invasive detail, the rude importunate matters of fact. They answered the phone and the door. They sorted mail. There was an intricate hierarchy of rank, a jockeying for position that evoked nothing so much as a Provençal court—who was in favor, who out, who had known Jimmy longer or better or where, who would do the shopping or join him in Paris for the television interview or help with the book-jacket photo. He was working, again, on a novel: *If Beale Street Could Talk.*

Jimmy drank scotch. We drank wine. I have not as yet described the quality of kindness in his manner, the affection he expected and expressed. His face is widely known—that dark glare, broad nose, those large protruding eyes, the close-fitting cap of curls then starting to go white. But photographs cannot convey the mobile play of feature, the intensity of utterance, the sense he could contrive to give that attention *matters* and gesture can count. There was something theatrical in Baldwin's manner, and it grew automatic at times. He would embark on what seemed a tirade, a high-speed compilation of phrases that clearly had been phrased before, a kind of improvised lecture spun out of previous speech. He stared at you unblinkingly; you could not turn away. He wore expensive jewelry and fingered it, talking; he smoked. He had been holding center stage for years.

You shifted in your seat. You said, "Yes, but . . ." and he raised his imperious manicured hand. Dialogue, for Baldwin, was an interrupted monologue; he would yield the platform neither willingly nor long. He could speak incisively on a book he had not read. But again and again he impressed me with his canny ranging, his alert intelligence. "Understand me," he would say. "It's important that you understand." And it was important, and you understood.

My pleasure in our meetings is easily explained. Here was the spokesman of his generation and color speaking directly to me. That he took my opinions seriously, that he read and respected my work, or appeared to, that he wanted us with him as often as possible—all this was flattering. When we parted, late at night, Jimmy would say, "See you two tomorrow." If we came for lunch instead, he urged us to stay on for dinner; when a friend passed through Saint-Paul, he would insist we meet.

Why he wanted to be with us is, I think, less clear. Each friendship partakes of the reciprocal trade agreement, and I can only speculate as to Baldwin's motives in the trade. He was the most sociable of solitaries; though constantly attended and attended to, he seemed nonetheless alone. He wanted to hear "news from home." Elena had worked several years in a rehabilitation agency for drug addicts in New York, whose clientele was largely black; she moved easily through his old streets. Though she was without exception the single woman in his house—and in a party of a dozen men—she was given pride of place. She sat at his right hand. They liked each other, I believe, with unfettered immediate liking; she treated him with just the right mixture of impatience and respect. They embraced each other, meaning it; they huddled in corners together. There was nothing exclusionary about his attitude to women; though surrounded by adoring boys he was also a "family man."

I mattered to him, I suppose, as a practitioner of a shared trade. He told me he was starved for the chance to talk books, for a discussion, say, of Henry James with someone who had read him. We talked the way most writers do, in a kind of shorthand and sign language. We asked each other, always, how the work had gone that day, how this paragraph was doing, or that character and scene.

Jimmy's acolytes believed the process sacramental, as if behind his workroom door strange rituals took place. He would shut himself into his study at midnight and somehow produce an object to which accrued money and fame. They had little sense, I think, of how much it was costing him to keep them all in style, of the anxious private wrangling in the watches of the night. His acclaim had diminished of late, and he knew I knew it. The alchemy of which his friends were confident was less mysterious to me and therefore more compelling; he worked at continual risk. And I was moved by his intensity, his struggle with a form that had come to seem elusive. *Beale Street* is not as finely honed as *Go Tell It on the Mountain* or *Giovanni's Room.* Yet writers must invent the wheel each time they start to write. That Baldwin had been consequential to a multitude of readers made all of this more poignant; he had made himself the benchmark to be passed.

Much of what I knew of the plight of the black American I had learned from reading him. And what sometimes seemed like paranoia could be argued as flat fact. The deaths of Malcolm X, of Medgar Evers, Martin Luther King, Bobby Kennedy, George Jackson, the named and nameless legion in what he called "the royal fellowship of death," his own impending fiftieth birthday, the increasing sickness of a beloved friend and mentor, Beauford DeLaney—all weighed heavily that winter. "This face," he'd say, and frame it with his slender glinting fingers. "Look at this crazy face."

In the early 1970s Nixon reigned unchallenged. The Watergate scandal was building but the hearings had not started yet. Each day brought more darkness to light. The French took corruption for granted, but we were transfixed. One litmus test for national allegiance, perhaps, has to do with political scandal. We rushed out for the paper and listened to the shortwave daily, but a "smoking gun" or upheaval in the political affairs of France could trigger no equivalent concern.

We waited like literal exiles for the summons to return. We discussed America with the fervor of the unrequited lover, curdling into scorn. We went for walks; we dawdled over drinks; we visited each other ("Hey, baby, what's up?" "Hey, darlin', where've you *been?*") gladly and often those months.

We had been at his house in Saint-Paul-de-Vence two or three times in a row; it was our turn, therefore, to invite the Baldwin clan. We did so, one Thursday, for lunch. They said they would come, happily; they were seven, maybe nine. The two members of his party I remember as men passing through were a dancer called Bertrand and a publisher named Willi. The former was lean, lithe, beautiful, and black; he danced at the Folies Bergère. The latter was mountainous, white. We had been warned about his appetite by Baldwin's cook days before; Willi was a voracious eater who had sent her to the market three times that afternoon.

Elena planned a *navarin;* we made an extra pot. A *navarin,* though simple, takes time to prepare; we started the previous day. We cubed the lamb and browned it, then fashioned the bouquet garni. We peeled turnips and carrots and leeks. Lilo Rosenthal knocked. She was hoping we might join her tomorrow for lunch; there were people she thought we should meet. We made our excuses, invited her in; as she could see we, too were preparing a meal. We would therefore be unable to join or invite her, for we owed a friend a thank-you *navarin.* I remember not naming his name. Part of this was inverse snobbery, a distaste for glitter by association, and part the suspicion that, had Lilo known Baldwin was coming, we should have had to invite her also. They would have been water and oil.

At any rate, she told us, she hoped we would take in our wash. It hung on the clothesline outside. She wanted to walk by the house and let her friends take photographs; they were passionate photographers. Her friends were distinguished, she said. They were the last of the Hapsburgs and the last of the Hohenzollerns, respectively. Or perhaps they were the last of the Schleswigs and Holsteins, or collateral branches instead. In any case they were old and distinguished and would not appreciate the laundry on our line. She hoped we would ready the house.

We promised. We made the second *navarin,* brought an extra dozen bottles from the *cave,* bought three additional *boules* from the baker, and waited for Jimmy to come. He himself did not drive. He had, however, purchased a brand-new Mercedes, dark brown and substantial, just short of stretch-limousine size. His driver would be working that day, he had assured me, they had no need of the little tattered *prinz*. He was bringing Bertrand, Daro, Philippe, Billy, Willi, and Bernard.

At the appointed hour we were ready; a car came. The day was overcast. What pulled into the parking space behind *le grand bassin* was not Jimmy's Mercedes but an ancient gray Renault. It was followed, funereally, by a Deux Chevaux. Lilo Rosenthal appeared. Her guests emerged. They were slow and small and bent. The process of arrival took some time. The doors opened, faltered, closed. The last of the Hapsburgs and the last of the Hohenzollerns wore dark suits and carried cameras and advanced with umbrellas and canes. They shuffled off together to Les Neiges. They kissed one another's hands.

As soon as they were out of sight we heard another car. The deep-throated growl of gears, the high hum of power in harness, the trumpeting bravura of the horn—and Baldwin's Mercedes roared up. It spat the raked gravel; it rocked on its brakes; it fairly pirouetted in the sudden sun. Four doors flung wide in unison; our company had come.

They were dressed for the occasion, grandly. They wore boaters and foulards. Their boots gleamed. Bertrand especially was splendid; he emerged twirling his scarf and waist-sash of pink silk. He did a few dance steps and flung his hat high and extended his hands for applause. We applauded. Jimmy embraced us; we him. The chauffeur was not happy with the switchbacks of the entry drive. "They're badly banked," he said. He had brought his lunch along and elected to stay with the car. He stood, arms folded, glowering down through the olive groves; he was Danish, thick and stolid and impervious to charm. "What a charming place," the publisher proclaimed. We piloted them in.

This was not easy; they swarmed. They raced to the crest of the meadow and walked tiptoe along the rim of the *bassin.* They approved the view. They clattered through our little house, exclaiming at the style of it, posing on the bedroom balcony. "Give me the simple life," they chorused. "Let's have *la vie en rose.*" Philippe had brought flowers; he garlanded Elena, Daro, Jimmy, Willi, and Bertrand. We emptied four bottles of wine by the time we settled to eat.

The *navarin* was a success. The publisher, Willi, approved. Audibly, he sighed; he sat back and rolled up his sleeves. "Which pot's for me?" he asked. There were olives and pâté. There was much laughter, celebration, praise for the salads and bread. The dining room could barely contain us; we rolled about the table like a litter of puppies suckling, jostling, slicing sausages and cheese and fruit and cake. A shadow appeared at the window. I looked up. Lilo Rosenthal was outside by the car. She and her four companions were inching to the house. They had their cameras at shoulder level, focusing, and it pained them, clearly, to approach.

We must have looked, to them, like Spengler's nightmare realized: the decline of the west. The beaming black man at the center, the lithe array around him, the voluminous white man with loaves in his hands, the young hosts plying everyone with wine, the pyramid of bottles, the ruckus of festivity, the Mercedes being polished—all this was hard to focus on or frame. I could see Lilo explaining.

I do not know how she explained. There was no laundry, however. They circled warily. We did not invite them in. They moved to the back of the house.

As winter lengthened into spring, we had visitors. It doubles the pleasure in place to show it to a first-time guest; we went often to our now familiar haunts. We visited, again, the Léger Museum in Biot, the Musée Picasso at Antibes. We admired the intricate functional ballet of workers at the glassworks, the Verrerie in Biot—the boys in shorts, wearing sneakers and goggles, manipulating molten glass and dancing from furnace to basin. The skilled ones made pitchers and bowls.

We bought pottery once more at the Madoura, Picasso's famed ceramic works. We took my editor, Jim Landis, for a fiery drive to Saint-Tropez; we ate celebratory dinners in Mougins and Magagnosc. When the mistral, with frost in its fist, pummeled the shutters and raked the bare oak branches down the roof of the small house, we scanned the dawn horizon for Corsica reflected; the nighttime lights of Grasse seemed closer than before.

Increasingly, we kept to the hills. We felt ourselves entitled now to disapprove of the tourist-choked Croisette. We went to the Carleton Hotel in Cannes for cocktails, or to the film festival, and could scarcely wait to escape. We preferred Gourdon to Nice, the harsher landscape to the manicured; we complained, in concert with the Levasseurs, that things were not as they *should* be or as they'd been before. I took pleasure in my *vieille voiture,* its shabby dented body and local license plates.

This stay had less to do with young love or first honeymoon than with willed endurance: the hard apartness of Provence. I would not have put it this way then, but the landscape mirrored mood. We came to terms with repetition, habit-rounds. Change seemed less important than earned consistency. We were loss-haunted a little and wondering how to go on.

Maija Bechstein wondered this aloud. She had moved into Alexander's *ruine.* It had been nearly finished while he lived; he had wanted it to be her wedding gift. They were married in the hospital, however, and had not shared the house. She was completing it less out of devotion than inertia; there seemed nothing else to do. Her first husband had renounced her; her children were estranged. The Swiss society she had violated by divorce would not accept her back. A neighbor there informed her that justice had been done: her lover's death was retribution, and she deserved to grieve.

Maija repeated this, her gray eyes wide. "It's so wicked," she said, "so lacking in, how do you call it, charity? Why must everybody always be unkind? I don't mean you, of course. You loved him. He loved you."

We came to love her too. She was a small-boned strong-nosed woman with curly gray-brown hair. She spoke a pell-mell mixture of English and German and French. Her voice was soft, her manner self-effacing. She was utterly bereft. I had not known before, and have not seen equaled since, such passion in an adult; she revered the memory of Alex unalloyed. He had spoken of her, earlier, with the same devotion. But "star-crossed lovers" are usually young, and there was something disconcerting in the case of these sixty-year-olds—a proper Swiss matron weeping, not bothering to wipe her tears, when she spoke of her dead darling who had been her husband for weeks. She adored him, she said, at first sight. Two years earlier, he had said the same of her. It was a *coup de foudre* for them both. We never saw them together, and their time together was brief. Yet Maija—sturdily striding beside us in the marketplace in Grasse, discussing the piano room he had envisioned and how to get a piano up the stairs, offering chocolate or cassis or talking of her childhood in Sumatra—seemed a woman stunned, a figure torn from tapestry or the lais of Marie de France.

I came to see her that way, anyhow. She compelled attention by her very lack of trying to, her refusal to complain. Had she to do it over again, she would have done it again. She regretted only that they did not meet sooner, that they had not run off together the first afternoon. He had been her Tristan, and she was his Isolde.

Music mattered to Maija, and she played the piano daily. "Perhaps I could give music lessons here," she said. "As soon as the piano room is finished. As soon as I find students." Then she would frown and chew her lip and rearrange the cutlery. "As soon as I am decent for an hour at a time."

She could not keep from weeping for that long. A

smell or turn of phrase or memory assaulted her; the knight who rode into her life had been unhorsed by cigarettes. His fine body lay in an urn. She had chosen to leave Switzerland—her husband, children, society, friends—for a man in mortal sickness, though they did not know that then.

Had she known it, she insisted, she would have left in any case; she would have gone with full awareness of the price to pay. Because the days she had with Alex were invaluable, and the days she had without him did not count. She spoke this way. It is a paraphrase but not distortion of the way she spoke. Her lack of ease with English helped, no doubt, to foster this sense of the romantic—the archaic turns of phrase, the involuntary directness: "My heart is broken. It is in two parts. He has buried one of them. I cannot repair my heart."

We gave a tea party on April 1. We invited four couples—all elderly, all European—to the little house. They had entertained us often, turn by turn; it was our chance to reciprocate. We bought patisserie by the box-full, tarts and fruit and cake. They were engineers and brokers and retired chemists, grave and kindly citizens, courtly men with stiff-brimmed hats, the women wearing gloves.

What imp of the perverse possessed me I can no longer tell. But it came to me, preparing, that this was April Fool's Day and we should observe it; we could introduce them to the time-honored custom of practical jokes. "A custom better honored in the breach," Elena said, and I said, no, we ought to do it, it would be terrific fun. We would start the meal with joke food and then repair to the real treats that waited covered on the sideboard or in the chill *cave.*

So we did the whole thing wrong—preparing coffee and tea, then spicing it, pouring vinegar in wine and pepper in the chocolate sauce, adding mustard to the jam. All the uproarious tricks of a ten-year-old returned to me—the whoopee cushion, the preshredded napkin, salt in the sugar bowl, dirt on the fork. I could scarcely contain my excitement; it seemed like the most fun in years.

When they arrived, we were waiting. We were mannerly, polite. We showed them the house, the flowers, the grounds; we discussed the weather and the circumstance of Watergate and how innocent the American people were as to corruption, how we failed to take it for granted, making molehill-mountains out of fraud and greed. They said that we were lucky, marvelously fortunate, and that youth— ourselves excepted, *naturellement*—is wasted on the young.

We sat. We offered wine, cake, and tea. Tittering, I poured while Elena cut and served. They tasted the first mouthful, expressionless, then ate. I had been waiting for the burst of laughter, the telltale recognition, dawning joke, the way we'd grin and explain it away, the proper feast to come.

Instead, and to my horror, they proceeded with the meal. They said how skilled we were, how domestically practiced; they even asked Elena for the recipe. "Where did you learn to cook?" one woman inquired—at whose house we had consumed a splendid six-course supper just the week before. Her question did not sound sarcastic. She drank the undrinkable brew. When her husband asked for seconds, I had had enough. I said the joke was over now, my little game was stupid, they did not need to continue. The cake was inedible, clearly; my own piece lay untouched.

"*Mais non,*" they said. "Don't be unkind. It's an excellent *gâteau.*"

"*Gâté,*" I said. "It's spoiled. We made it this way on purpose. It's April Fool's, you see."

"April Fool's?"

"The first of April. *Un gâteau gâté*—a spoiled cake. On this day we play practical jokes."

"How sweet of you," they said, "to make excuses for your wife. But she doesn't require them, truly. She will learn to bake."

"She knows it already," I said.

"How very sweet."

"How gallant. *Les jeunes mariés.*"

"I'll have some more," said the excellent cook, "of your excellent coffee. *Merci.*"

I have not played an April Fool's joke since.

The Levasseurs, little by little, introduced us to the servants on the neighboring estates. It was an education. That "no man is a hero to his valet" may be a cliché, but I had not encountered the valets of heroes before. And in that wet, dank winter the owners stayed away; they would not take up residence till May. So we picnicked on the grounds of houses that had wrought-iron gates; we joined in games of *boules* behind the stable that now served as a garage. Together with the gardeners and cooks and the chauffeur, we used the swimming pools.

Lord and Lady B., for instance, served in India. They were now in their eighties and kept themselves hearty by walks. They were in Bermuda visiting the children the day we tried their pool. The Levasseurs brought pizza prepared in the Provençal manner; we furnished wine. Germain and Michele brought the cheese and the fruit and cold chicken and quiche; the cook for Lord and Lady B. produced hot food. She was estranged from the butler. They had been very close, Felicity confided; you understand me, Nicholas, extremely close. Her face lit up with the signal joy of gossip; now they are arguing and then they will be close again, you'll see.

There was a great deal of silver. The butler sat in the dining room, polishing trophies and trays. He had completed the cups. I asked him how often he did this, and he said, continually; he would no sooner finish the flatware and the serving spoons than the candelabra would begin to tarnish once again. He polished two hours a day. He was wearing a blazer and bow tie; he had a waxed moustache. His blazer pocket bore a regimental badge. He spoke of India with fondness and regret. Everything was different then, not better for everybody, mind you, I'm not saying that. But it was better for me.

The cook appeared. She switched off the light.

"Henri, you *must* join us," she said. "Don't be a silly baby." Her breasts were large, her stomach ample, her hair in curlers; she put her hand on his neck. She fondled his bald spot. He blushed.

Their reconciliation pleased us all. We were shown the bedrooms of Lord and Lady B. We admired the mirrors, the gold plate on the faucet taps, the closets full of dress clothes, and the citation from the queen. There was a signed photograph of Mountbatten and many portraits of young women looking solemn, wearing white. They looked at the photographer with bright disdainful eyes.

We played cards and drank and swam. I asked if Lady B. enjoyed the pool. The butler was raucous by now; he had changed into a bathing suit and sat holding hands with the cook. He said, she swims like this—and vigorously bobbed his head, exhaling through pursed lips. Germain the driver said, "You must see it. I'll show you." He disappeared inside. They laughed. Felicity and Guillaume were dozing on deck chairs in the increasing heat. Then Germain emerged with a brassiere. He held it by the straps—enormous, pink. "Give it to me," the butler said. He tied it round his head, as if the cups were earmuffs, and teetered to the diving board. They whistled, clapped, and urged him on; he jumped.

The daybook lists long days of rain. Maija, at our dining table, spoke brokenly of Alex and his cat called Wednesday—found as a stray on a Wednesday—who disappeared in Nice. There were stories of men drowned along the Corniche, swept out to sea by the current. There were stories of arson and drugs. *Le Figaro* and *Nice-Matin* showed photographs of corpses or the starlets mobbed at Cannes. The elderly were everywhere about us, limping through the cobbled streets or sitting on benches to wait for a bus. Each morning, emptying the coal ash, I looked at the Pré-Alpes to see if that night's rain had brought snow to the mountains and how far down was white.

Elena was not well. She went to a series of doctors for tests; they took x-rays and analyzed blood. They suggested a healthful glass of Burgundy or goat's milk; they commended exercise and drugs. They prescribed exploratory surgery and chamomile tea and many of the stages in between. She did not drink the potions nor submit to surgery. The pain proved bearable, and then it went away.

There are two church bells audible from Les Neiges d'Antan. One is the steeple in Châteauneuf-de-Grasse and one in Opio. They do not agree as to time. The chimes from Châteauneuf are set three minutes earlier than those of Opio; they complete their ringing before the neighbor begins. The first French round I learned in school cursed the bell ringer sonorously.

God created the bell ringer, we sang, in order to make the singer miserable; he scratches at the bells and pulls

the rope from dawn to dusk. When will those busy, noisy
bells ring the death of the ringer himself?

> *Maudit sois tu, carillonneur*
> *Que Dieu créa pour mon malheur.*
> *Dès le point du jour, à la cloche il s'accroche,*
> *Et le soir encore, carillonne plus fort.*
> *Quand sonnera-t-on la mort du sonneur?*

This dislocation was made manifest every fifteen
minutes. At night it could keep me awake. The keepers of
the clocks were rigid with their rectitude, but one was
surely wrong. When Châteauneuf rang midnight, it remained—in Opio—the end of the previous day. Which of
the clocks was accurate? I asked myself, and had no way of
knowing. True time lay between.

IX

✳

1987

The children have been singing through Avignon and Nîmes and down the busy avenues to the Pont du Gard. They are resolutely cheerful, intoning nonsense rounds. Linda teaches them. "On the lonesome prairie, where nature favors no man, a buffalo and his brother were lying in the sand. *In the sand.*"

A man in a white bird costume has entertained us at lunch. A little mad, perhaps, but mostly canny and tricked out to please, he pedals up and arranges his musical props. He has a guitar, a flute, harmonica, bells and wind chimes and a toy drum; his nose is pronounced, his face closely shaven. He wears white feathers fashioned out of bed sheets and a turban, also white. His bicycle is festooned with drapery; a large Latin sign balanced on the handlebars proclaims "All that lives is love." He wields a dragon from Tarascon and serenades us abstractedly, as if preoccupied. Later, leaving town, we see him also leaving, his bicycle and gear stowed safely in the backseat of a blue Renault, looking every inch the salesman heading to his next appointment or home for a siesta or on to the *bureau*. Though Andrea waved and whistled at him, he did not respond. We lost him at Villeneuve-lès-Avignon.

Men sell fresh-squeezed orange juice for fifty francs

a bottle at the Pont du Gard; Agrippa's pipeline pours out hikers through its dry stone mouth, a conduit for flesh. We walk where water ran. There are babies with ice cream in the cafés, dogs lifting their legs on the chairs. In the green river underneath, people swim and paddle kayaks and canoes. Planes split the sky here palpably, the pride of France aloft.

More than twice the age I was when I first lived in France, I have changed more than the landscape, no matter how the knowing locals complain that the landscape has changed. When François I decreed all the Vaudois should die, when the village of Lourmarin and the surrounding towns were corrected via extinction, that rock outcrop caught the southwest sun as it does this afternoon; those olive trees lifted, glinting, as they do today. A disbeliever gets enlightened, said a cynic of the time, by lightening; we remove, for the good of the patient and in the interest of immortal health, the festering locus of doubt, to wit, the head. The followers of Pierre Valdo—except for those Vaudois who fled uninstructed to Italy—shall be slaughtered, therefore saved.

Andrea and I pick flowers, at the neighbor's invitation, from her well-kept flower beds. There are roses and marigolds, zinnias, impatiens, mumms; there are pansies and lilies and cyclamen and hydrangea. I am struck by my ability to recognize these plants—not because my knowledge is extensive but because they are so similar to flowers in Vermont. There are certain climatic equivalencies here; New York shares a latitude with Nice.

We picnic in the *forêt de cèdres*, under a lowering sky. Other families do too. The road that used to lead to Oppède-le-Vieux has been barred to prevent further destruction and the risk of forest fires; so the sign affirms. Brigitte, the postmistress—an open-faced, pretty woman with strawberry marks festooning her arms—is here with her children. We wave. They have a poodle, yipping, high-pitched, a bow at its neck. I think of my vast placid dog at home: Major Scobie, one hundred and forty pounds of black panting devotion, his tail a threat to countertops, his head the poodle's size.

A goat escaped from the villa below and found its way to our house. Looking in the windows at its own reflection, it seemed to think it had regained the herd. Bleating piteously, it waited by the window. And when I closed the shutter, closing down the mirror, it found the next reflection. *"Elle est mignonne,"* our neighbor said. *"Elle n'est pas du tout sauvage.* She's gentle, she's not at all wild." Still, we could not catch her. She capered and leaped down the rock wall, evasive, a creature unused to no cage.

The Abbaye de Senanques is beautifully situated and well restored and maintained. It hosts an exhibition devoted to a kind of comparative religion survey, to the proposition that all men worship, though the forms of worship change. So there is a photograph of Buddha and a panel display of

whirling dervishes and a picture of the synagogue in Cavaillon. Indians and Africans are pictured at their rites. One
cannot but endorse the humanistic tidings and the humane
message offered on the placards, but it feels hypocritical.
The not-so-subtle subtext is, "See these charming heathen
at their play." And think of the stern, silent men who built
this monastery once, their inflexible rigor. A Cistercian
abbey devoted to comparative religion makes a nearly
comic contradiction in terms. They sell lavender soap and
devotional music and books about Provence and honey in
the entryway; they have a concert series and blue folding
chairs.

There is a present craze for "personalized" trin-
kets—combs or cups or key rings with their owner's name
attached. So in America you find a rack of coffee mugs
reading Adam, Alan, Alice, Bill, and Bob. The names are
plentiful and various; children ratify themselves by reading
how they've made the list: Ed, Eileen, Ellen, and so forth.
In England and France we also found ourselves hunting
cups, and one might deduce—with no other evidence—the
country from the rack. Here market research reinforces
rather than eradicates distinction; in England the teacups
had been incised Adrian, Anthony, Charles, Diana, Dun-
can, Geoff and Nigel, names that would require a special
order in America or France. We stand before a wheel of
cups in Moustiers-Sainte-Maries. The wheel bristles with
names that could not be other than French: André, Ariane,
Chantal, Dominique, Eloise. There are Danielle and Phil-
lippe and Gerard, Jacques and Jeanne, Marie-Hélène. By
their titles ye shall know them, and the little rim of flowers
at the lip.

The Crédit Agricole sits next to the Foyer Rural. Then there comes the post office, the pharmacy, an antique shop and restaurant; then the village ends. This street is shaded by plane trees, and beyond there is a soccer field and meadow and then the Château de Lourmarin rising. Horses graze. One day we take our usual walk to the market and post office, but the street has been roped off. Children with buckets of paint and long chalk sticks have claimed it; they decorate the pavement with color bursts and stars and gaudy beasts and Cheshire cats in trees. There are perhaps fifteen artists, from five to ten years old; three women supervise. These three contrive to look soignée in paint-spattered jeans.

One girl has drawn a dinosaur. Its tail is red, neck purple, teeth and claws bright yellow; it breathes green fire and looks both domestic and fierce. Though the body is a dinosaur's, the head belongs on a dragon. We watch her embellish this shape. It is ten or twelve feet long, with scales along its body and ineffectual spears dangling from its lifted tail and warriors fleeing while others aim arrows—stick-figured antagonists, dwarfed. She has talent and precision; her companions provide her with paint.

Her name is Janine, I learn, because the women call to her. "Hey-ho," they clap their hands. "Janine!" She pays them no attention. She is working on the forward foot, *Tyrannosaurus* rampant, making shapes beneath the claw that look like gouts of blood. The light is bright. The plane-tree leaves give mottled shade, and the breeze gives motion; the painted creatures on the street seem therefore poised to move. They lumber down the concrete glade, advancing through leaf-shadow. Oil stains on the tarmac form their iridescent eyes.

"Is this an art class?" Cesca asks.

"A club?" Andrea asks.

We are not invited to join. There is coherence, clearly, to this group. They move west as if by prearrangement; they decorate the street in front of the antique dealer, then the restaurant. One woman takes a brush and deftly, sketchily, provides the outline of a panther. A small child paints it black. The paint dries quickly, gleaming. Janine continues with her herd of dinosaur-dragons and the warriors (their quivers empty, their arrows broken) in flight and disarray. The one who drew the panther is her mother, possibly; they look alike. They are dark, lush, wide-hipped, focused: women of the tribe. They work as if in concert, with no wasted motion; we might be at Lascaux once more, in the lamp-lit cave.

Good King René has been much celebrated for his several attainments. Scholar, poet, painter, linguist, and musician, he was the light of the court. Duke of Anjou, Count of Provence, and King of Naples and Sicily, he died in 1480, at the age of seventy-two; he knew Greek, Latin, Italian, Catalan, and Hebrew, geology and law. Henry James, describing *A Little Tour in France,* found King René attractive. "He was both clever and kind," James avers, "and many reverses and much suffering had not embittered him nor quenched his faculty of enjoyment. He was fond of his sweet Provence, and his sweet Provence has been grateful; it has woven a light tissue of legend around the memory of Good King René."

He studied mathematics and muscatel grapes and married Isabelle of Lorraine when he was twelve years old; two years after her death, he married Jeanne de Laval. They face each other on the panels of *The Burning Bush*, Nicholas Froment's triptych in the Cathédrale de Saint Sauveur in Aix.

The king kneels on the left-hand side and Jeanne de Laval the right. Her face looks smart and severe. His is bulbous nosed and strong jawed and not handsome, a face one still might see at the *tabac*, or driving a taxi, or drinking pastis. The later statue by David d'Angers, where the king holds the grapes he brought to the region, seems more prepossessing; it surveys the east end of the cours Mirabeau. But Nicholas Froment knew his subject, and there is blood and bone beneath the royal gown.

They are working on the cathedral, repairing the old baptistry; there is much litter and dust. I cannot find *Le Buisson Ardent*, though I remember it with clarity from years before. When asked for its location, the attendant does not know. I ask for the picture of Good King René, and she understands about René but does not know the picture; her business is floors. She is friendly, however—apologetic, even—and she conducts me to a black woman stacking chairs. She knows about King René also, but not the burning bush; she knows, however, that Marielle will know.

Marielle is getting brooms. Marielle will return in a

minute. I look about again and, in the cloister, meet Marielle; she has three brooms under her arm. She is red haired and voluble and anxious to assist me, but she does not know. There is, however, a map. On the map of the cathedral I locate the triptych and find its site in the aisle. It has been closed, the side panels folded over and, meeting in the center, padlocked shut.

A tour guide points at the ceiling, speaking German to her group. She laments the impropriety of juxtaposition, the fourteenth-century belfry, the sixteenth-century Gothic nave, the very early baptistry (Merovingian, fifth century), and the Roman columns and Renaissance cupola; this gallimaufry of periods has neither distinction nor unity but nonetheless a certain charm. Her German is meticulous and her accent poor. It is, I remember, bad taste in the French to speak with a good German accent. I had very much wanted to see the Froment, its celebration of virginity, the castles of Beaucaire and Tarascon precisely rendered in the background, the clear-eyed inclusion of detail that persuades far more than can abstraction as to the painter's homage. The dozen Germans advance on the nave. The men have been to Barbados or Hawaii on a previous trip; they wear shirts with pineapples and patterns of coconut palms.

At the entrance to the cathedral a man sits, legs tucked under, cap held out. If you are a Christian, he says, if you believe in God then give me money, please. I am not and I do not and I will not, I tell him; the locked triptych has made me argumentative. Curse you—he hoists himself up on his knees—what business did you have in there anyhow, defiling it? His curses are ingenious and lengthy,

cleansing in their high-pitched hum. By the time I'm out of
earshot I feel fine.

The Atelier Cézanne is open, on the hill now called the
avenue Paul Cézanne. He died in 1906, and the rooms have
been reconstituted to look like ones he labored in; there are
bottles and bowls and skulls, as in his sketches, and a sheaf
of books. There is a high wooden easel and brushes as if just
set aside while the artist used the toilet or went for a smoke
or a walk. There are apples and bananas and oranges and
lemons in the clusters he made famous. There are apples
drying and onions on the sill. They have shriveled greatly,
and Cesca says maybe these were his actual apples, they look
as if they've waited long enough.

Cézanne came from prosperous stock, and he could
seem disreputable to family members in Aix. There is a
story that Rodin, who never worked in marble, kept a
smock covered with marble chips and white dust in his
studio. When customers came to visit he would greet them
in his smock, with marble dust on cheek and beard, so as
to comply with their expectation of the artist in fine frenzy
toiling, chisel and mallet in hand. In fact he worked with
wax. In fact Cézanne was the most methodical of workmen,
the *bourgeois primitif,* and this mess feels contrived.

In the Musée Granet in Aix, they show some of the
paintings that he studied when apprenticed there, canvases
he copied or found himself influenced by. And there would
seem to be no doubt—though the point is stretched, at

times—that he *did* copy canvases and themes. How else does one acquire earned originality than by influence absorbed? The artist must have models, and they may as readily be canvas as still life or flesh. The model may well be a previous master—a host of teachers and their work—as much as a girl without clothes.

In this sense, then, the meaning of *derivative* argues legacy. We need something from which to derive. It is a declension of sorts, a handing on. So too with innovation. A primary meaning, according to the *Oxford English Dictionary*, is "the alteration of what is established by the introduction of new elements or forms." For the imagination, however, a botanical use of the term comes closer to the mark: "The formation of a new shoot at the apex of a stem or branch; esp. that which takes place at the apex of the thallus or leaf-bearing stem of mosses, the older parts dying off behind; also . . . a new shoot thus formed." Now Mont Sainte Victoire is famous because of how often the artist observed it; on the *autoroute* they point an arrow at the mountain, saying *Pays de Cézanne.*

It is not so much, as Wilde suggests, that the sunset's a second-rate Turner as that nature takes on Turner's guise while the sky changes color at night. So too with Cézanne's still lifes and mountains in the changing light; they define the landscape that they were once defined by. No single field of sunflowers fails to remind us of van Gogh. No brown-skinned fruit-bearing sarong-wrapped beauty seems other than Gauguin's.

The cruel irony of van Gogh's fame grows yearly more apparent; he could not sell those canvases at cost that now sell for tens of millions of dollars. Alive he was ignored and dead revered. Reputations are subject to fashion; X may be overvalued, Y undersold. But there is no example with which I am familiar that feels as extreme. Part of this painter's despair came from the simple lack of recognition, creature comforts, the fear that no commercial person other than his brother would take him seriously. And it's not of course self-evident that he could have been happy if rich—less subject to self-doubt or rage, less tormented, longer lived. Perhaps he might not have dealt with good fortune as fruitfully as bad; perhaps he painted at such speed because he had a sense of his allotted time. This is a critical commonplace as to genius extinguished young. Mozart or Schubert composed in haste because they knew they could not do so at reflective length; Keats wrote at fever pitch because of his wasting disease . . .

In any case we do not, cannot know. Yet van Gogh and Gauguin and Cézanne were in no sense precocious; they struggled for attainment, line by line. Their work was all hard earned. Now, for an entrance fee, we get to see—from windows and on bookshelves—what Cézanne once saw.

Another site, now largely rubble, has the magic in it. At Wylie's written urging, we drive there for the day. The fort of Buoux commands the sightlines of the long coomb cut into the Lubéron that is the Lourmarin Gap. This was accomplished, over millenia, by the torrential Aigue-Brun—though it is hard to see that silted trickle, this present shallow river, as a chisel on the cliffs. Its water cut so steeply, once, that nothing grows.

The rock canyon meanders, roughly, north to south. It is the way to travel if you have to travel through. There are cliff faces and men practicing on them; they work in teams, with ropes. We walk beneath rock overhangs and slowly up the hillside to the fort of Buoux. Ascending on what are labeled "Rupestrian" steps, we pass cisterns and silos, the silos also cisterns, hollowed out of rock. One of them still has its stone cover in place. I try to lift it, cannot.

The children are excited. There are sheer drops all around. They edge as close to edges as we will allow, then insist we look; the view is always better from this next particular perch. In the distance, astonishingly, lavender flourishes—a bright planted purple rectangle, with the yellow of sunflowers still farther off. In the hamlet that is Buoux itself, a portable radio blares; the town of Marseilles supports a vacation campsite by the river, and a celebration is in progress. The decibel level seems astonishing, as does the distance laughter carries. We are miles away. The "Rupestrians" lived in hollowed-out sections of hill. We skirt them. There are ramparts up above.

We take pictures of the view. We take pictures of one another in the view. Linda takes a picture of us all. There are arches and the wreckage of a church and gate (from Celtic to Roman to medieval structure equally in rubble) and fortified positions rising up to the cliff's crest. The last of these is a dungeon. Those who were imprisoned could escape only by literal flight; the drop looks absolute. There is scrub and thistle and wind on the white rock. From the summit's vantage you can watch the four directions.

When François I came down to instruct the Vaudois in legitimacy, he put two thousand people to death; those few who could escape most probably did so through here. On February 1, 1545, he ordered that the countryside be *"dépeuplé et nettoyé,"* emptied and cleaned of those who had improper faith. They were hung, stoned, decapitated, and, in graphic French, "put to the point of the sword."

How few advance on forts, their hands held out or weaponless, carrying the olive branch and not the torch! How suspicious and warlike the question "Friend or foe?" A history this ancient puts matters in perspective; we have been slaughtering one another, or trying to, since history began. The fort of Buoux was leveled, as so much else, by Richelieu's decision to consolidate the kingdom and destroy what could oppose it. Our daughters, gazing down, say "Imagine if they threw you off, or if you were a prisoner, or what it would feel like to be here, in this dungeon. Imagine boiling oil!"

We flatter ourselves on how far we have come and how the warlike instinct has been brought to book. It means, I think, that we are lethal only at a distance—not less lethal as a species, and potentially far more. A hawk wheels beneath us, then dives. There is a high-pitched, briefly audible squeal. Then the music takes over again—the campers from Marseilles. Something stirs in the cistern's green scum. Like any parent I fear for my children, and my children's children, that they will inherit this wind.

We have a drink in Cucuron, a village five miles from our own. Elena orders coffee and I a pastis; we sit beneath a plane tree, on the square. The restaurant next door will open in an hour; the staff eat first. There are six of them, all young, at table; the men sit on one side, the women on the other. They take turns fetching food. They are raucous, happy with each other and the prospect of the evening, pals, *copains.* There are pitchers of wine. It took little time for us to recognize that they are staff, not customers; the disorderly abundance of the food, the way they disappear inside, the pace of the consumption—so that they eat more and more rapidly than those who pay—all this reveals intention. At the table next to ours a couple folds a map. They speak softly, in a language I can't place. The man is tall, white bearded, wearing sandals—sufficiently striking so that I remember having seen him some days earlier, on the path to the source of the Sorgues. Neither Cucuron nor Fontaine-de-Vaucluse are on the standard Cook's tour of Provence, and this couple therefore has its own itinerary, as do we. He too is drinking pastis. He raises his glass to me, smiles. I am gratified that he remembers us, as I do them: the momentary fellowship of strangers, for whom a twice-seen sight or face grows marginally less strange. We do not speak. He spreads the *Michelin* out on the table. His wife has a pencil; she traces the lines of their route.

The village square is dominated by a concrete pool. The pool is green, rectangular, and large. We cannot gauge the water's depth, since it is opaque. The wind has driven clutter—a floating bottle of Evian, some plastic wrappers, the plane trees' shed bark—down to the side where we sit. Children fish from the low wall. It is hard to imagine that fish live within or would prove edible if caught, but the timeless pleasure of dropping a line into darkness, of waiting with your hand held out for signals sent on string—this pleasure engages them wholly. They huddle and wait.

"A watched pot never boils," I think, might just as well mean the reverse. The standard explication of the saying is "Don't supervise too much" or "Leave the procedure alone." But milk for coffee should not boil or pea soup bubble over; in these cases one *should* watch. So perhaps "A watched pot never boils" means, contrarily, "Pay attention." The boys at the rim of the *bassin* pay close attention, anyhow—though what they catch are leaves.

We return to a menu our daughters have made and elegantly lettered, with flowers drawn between courses. The courses read: *"Compote de Fruit. Salade Verte. Soupe à l'Oignon. Carottes à la Nivernaise. Spaghetti à la Provençale. La Quiche Lorraine. Du Fromage. Du Dessert."* They have been planning this for days, have shopped in busy secrecy, then sent us off to Cucuron while they set the table; they have been cooking since noon. Linda oversees. They have rarely cooked before, and Cesca says she's sorry she can't manage meat. But they have learned to chop and slice and have worked out a schedule. In less elegant print, the duty chart reads: "They come at seven thirty. Andrea shows them up and Cesca brings drinks. Andrea leads them down to the table, Cesca brings fruit salad. Cesca clears fruit salad. Andrea brings green salad, Andrea clears green salad. Cesca brings onion soup, Cesca clears onion soup. Andrea brings carrots, Andrea clears carrots. Cesca brings spaghetti, Cesca clears spaghetti. Andrea brings quiche, Andrea clears quiche. Cesca brings cheese, Cesca clears cheese. We bring dessert and coffee and JOIN THEM."

They are conspiratorial, cackling in the kitchen. They have put on their best clothes. Andrea in particular, to whom pretense is earnest, acts as if she does not know us, as if we are valued customers only now arrived. Cesca curtsies and burbles and brings out dishes till ten; they have studied how to make a quiche and carrots *à la Nivernaise* from cookbooks in the house. Dessert is ice cream and cookies, and they take off their aprons and join us. It is a plenitude.

X

❋

1976

When next we settled at Les Neiges, it was with a daughter. My mother Barbara Delbanco, died in March of 1974; our first child, Francesca Barbara, was born at the end of that May. In 1975, we planned for a winter in Grasse. Lilo Rosenthal agreed, and the Levasseurs arranged to meet us at the airport once again.

Francesca fell ill at Kennedy Airport. She vomited all over herself, Elena's dress, our suitcases. We postponed the trip a day or two; the fever, however, remained. By the time she was well, we were ill; by the time we were ready to travel, it would have been too late to leave. We tried again next year, when Cesca was nineteen months old. The snow in New York was severe. We struggled to the airport; flights were delayed, then canceled. We left instead the next day. In retrospect these tribulations scarcely seem severe; they make the sort of anecdote each traveler can tell. And I mention them here merely because they represent stages of age: a trip to France with wife and daughter is a different proposition from flying there footloose, alone.

This time we borrowed Maija Bechstein's Deux Chevaux. She was staying in Switzerland for the winter and let us use the car. So the declension is complete: from

Alfa-Romeo to Deux Chevaux, from boy in a sports car to family man in a borrowed jalopy. I pass myself driving the Moyenne Corniche. I am the man on the right, the one hugging the inside lane, losing power on the climb, holding the wheel with both hands. I clench my teeth and shake my head and use the horn continually; the boy accelerates. He does not even notice that I brake.

We had been warned that the French did not sell plastic disposable diapers and that they would be hard to find in our small village stores. We puzzled over this. Elena did not want to hand-wash laundry daily, and we had no way of knowing if the warning was correct. So we sent five hundred diapers, a.b.s. Les Levasseurs, from a Sears catalogue outlet to Châteauneuf-de-Grasse. We did so three months in advance.

They had not arrived by the time we came, and the Superette sold diapers in ranked rows. This seemed a reasonable price to pay for our long-distance doubt; we bought French diapers instead. But then, long after we settled in and only days before we were scheduled to leave, I was informed by customs that our boxes had arrived. We would have left them there. But Guillaume disliked such waste and knew a baby who could profit from the diapers; therefore we went to La Bocca to claim the cartons from Sears.

The officials were suspicious. What would anyone wish with five hundred diapers from America when there were perfectly good ones—better, surely—available in France? It was a reprise of the baker's suspicion when Elena tried to imitate his *boules*. Why had we bothered to ship such redundancy, and was there not another reason—one hidden perhaps in the fabric itself, that multiplicatory fold of plastic that could disguise objects of interest to the authorities, themselves? In consequence we must permit them to open the boxes, examine the contents, to see what this peculiar shipment might mean. They were not born yesterday, these officers, they knew what we made of the French Connection and that it could be reversed; they were doing their duty, understand, their duty consisted of finding the culprit in five hundred diapers, the white contents thereof that could not surely and simply be plastic, don't take me please for a fool.

This is the place, perhaps, for the obligatory plaint about French bureaucrats. They are fiendish as to detail and devoted to minutiae and inefficient in the extreme. They sign and countersign and stamp and seal with relish; they are a nation of vendors convinced that you as customer are preparing to cheat on the purchase or have no right to buy. And heaven help the customer who cannot, in fact, afford the shop; the policeman does not find such poverty amusing. He reports to his superiors; superiors own shops.

French bureaucrats are scornful and incurious. They revel in their power and they do so in inverse proportion to rank; the more menial the position the more pompous its functionary. This is all the worse, surely, if one is a foreigner, but I believe the horrors of the system pertain to French nationals also. It is as if those men and women behind the glass partitions have labored so long to arrive in the sanctum that they must keep others back. They have abandoned all humor, not to mention hope. They will not smile. It is improper to smile. It is improper to have copies of the document; you must have the original. It is improperly filed. The file cabinet cannot be opened without the proper key. The supervisor has the key; the supervisor is in a meeting, monsieur, and cannot be disturbed.

And the very horror of the system perpetuates itself, doubling the workload, quadrupling the number of those who wait on line. Since every visit to an office takes, perforce, three visits, the arithmetic is clear.

Kafka is the poet of such madness, but the maze his creatures wander through looks dark or dimly lit. French lighting is superb. Everything is written, listed, organized, in order—but it fails to work. And in no other administrative system to which I have been subjected does one sense the whiff of cruelty, the tinge of xenophobic sadism. The English, for example, go about their tedious business with apologetic decency, the Indians with indifference, the Italians with improvisational flair. But the French have created a civil service so perfect it feeds on itself. It is perpetual motion; it requires no outside impetus to function, and any interference with its inward-facing smugness is to be ignored.

So they went through our five hundred diapers and let us, finally, go. Had Francesca not been with us, we would be waiting still. She proved our protectress in many such places; even the French bureaucrat takes pity on the young. The unbending ticket taker bent to take a ticket from her outstretched fist; the butcher's wife who faced me with stony suspicion on all our previous visits (he beat her,

Felicity said, if she so much as looked at other men) this time was wreathed in smiles. In an ancient Citroën, with a plump-cheeked porcelain-skinned baby, we were acceptable at last. We wheeled her through the market stalls in her portable orange stroller, and she came out clutching chocolate and ribbons and croissants.

But a price of admission lies hidden in every *entrée libre.* Though Jimmy sent a telegram when he learned of Cesca's birth *("Bravo pour la fillette!")*, there would be fewer late-night rambles through Saint-Paul-de-Vence. On our first stay in Opio, we heard Ike and Tina Turner at Le Club Valbonne; this winter there would be no nightclubs, no extended invitation to the dance. It was a quiet time. We stayed home or went for short walks. We ate hurried meals. At six o'clock each morning, I listened for her cry. Cesca was precocious and began to speak a kind of Franglais, but we knew no babysitters who spoke English. We could not bring ourselves to leave her—would not have wanted to, as doting first-time parents—at more than momentary length. We read Richard Scarry books and fairy tales and Ludwig Bemelmans on *Madeline;* we memorized, or so it seemed, much of Mother Goose.

The Levasseurs had a friend who loved hunting, particularly birds. He had perfected bird calls. He was grandfatherly, exuberant; he capered and whistled for fun. He made faces at Cesca, intending to amuse her; she was not amused. He imitated birds. This caught her attention; he flapped his arms and stood on his tiptoes and crowed. Thereafter she ran to him, expectant, while he ululated like a swallow, dove, or thrush. She called him, interchangeably, Mister Oiseau or Monsieur Bird. I did not tell her why his calls were so proficient or their true purpose: to flush out the quarry, then kill.

The Levasseurs adored her; she was *"notre jolie poupée."* They brought her sweets remorselessly and admired how "our pretty doll" clapped her hands or sat in the stroller as if giving audience or climbed the hill behind the house or did not cry when she fell. They praised her teeth, her fingers. They drove to Grasse and back *("Non, Nicolas, ce n'est rien")* to fill a prescription or to collect, as quickly as possible, a roll of developed film. She was a beauty, they proclaimed, she was angelic and brilliant and particularly wise. She had a knowledgeable stare, a *sagesse* that astonished, a patience and an understanding that was formidable, truly; we must send them pictures every birthday, every Christmas, so they might admire how she grows. They bought her frocks and sweaters a size too large, so that when we returned *chez nous* and required some souvenir, she would wear these clothes from France and perhaps remember . . .

I accompanied Guillaume to the Cave Cooperative. We bought wine *de douze degrés,* twelve percent. He approved of the local red and white, but not rosé; rosé brought on the migraine, he averred. It was too acid; he suffered in the evening if he drank rosé at lunch. The containers when full were too heavy for one man to lift. They held thirty liters apiece, dark green outsize bottles in wicker baskets with thick woven handles. We filled four at a time.

Then the process of decanting and distribution began. These vats were impractical for daily use; they had to be raised on a platform and siphoned off. We washed bottles of every description—used bottles, high-shouldered or sloped, in three-quarter or full liter sizes, even fruit-juice containers. Then Guillaume attached a hose. It was four feet long and pliable, pink. He presented me with the free end to suck, to establish the flow of the wine. When my mouth was full I nodded, and the siphoning began. This was rhythmic, pleasing work. One man inserted and pinched off the hose, the other placed the bottles and drove down the corks. There was little spillage, little waste. I would carry my share of the booty back to the cool *cave* behind the house. We would save the corks and wash out the containers after drinking, and then begin again.

We drove to Monaco. This time, instead of the casino, we visited the aquarium. We flapped our arms like fins; we made fish mouths, through the glass, at the circling fish. In Vallauris we admired the statue of the shepherd in the village square. Picasso had found refuge there in wartime France and, grateful, donated his *Shepherd* to the town. The figure is Attic in feeling, archaic, a man with a lamb in his arms. Cesca could identify the lamb. "How does the lamby go?" "Baa, baa, baa." "How does the kitty go?" "Meeow, meeow." "And how does Yucca go?" "Roof, ruf, yap."

It rained continually. On January 25, it snowed. The Alpes-Maritimes went white; the route Napoléon was closed. I redoubled my efforts with *la chaudière,* but there was something chill and inward to our visit this time through. Guillaume feared the olives would freeze. The *souches,* the frozen trunks, from the great freeze of '56 were a perpetual grief; the stumps reproached him still. He had not been employed as *gardien* then, or he might have intervened with drapery and fire. An olive tree grows slowly and cannot be replaced. You understand me, Nicholas, a lifetime is a few feet only to an olive tree. They are a reproach.

When we drove into the Var, or visited Fayence and Bargemon, or walked through the empty echoing spaces of l'Abbaye de Thoronet, we felt ourselves in touch with something more forbidding than the perfumed slopes of Grasse. It grew possible to see walled villages as a self-protective siting, not a photo opportunity. Cannes was growing year by year more tinselly and hectic; if imitation be the sincerest form of flattery, then we as Americans should have felt flattered by the modish coast.

Provence gives the semblance of plenty. Yet the tour buses came to seem like Trojan Horses by the narrow gate. It may be called a Roman gate or Gate of the Saracens; it keeps the tour buses back. They park in caparisoned rows. Inventive beyond Leonardo's imagination—he who sketched such intricate machinery of war—they raise a siege. They disgorge an army with credit cards and traveler's checks who are made welcome within. *"Timeo Danaos, et Dona ferentes,"* says Virgil's Laocoön. His warning was of course ignored; wily Odysseus was the first of the Greeks bearing gifts.

We filled our sack with pillage (gift crocks of herbes de Provence, a lemon-wood highchair, a prie-dieu, a large brass *laitier* with matching ladle, a number of copper pots and perfume samplers and olive-wood bowls and pottery from Moustiers and Fayence) and sent it to America; it was easier to send that booty out than to bring diapers in. So Les Neiges felt less and less like home and more a stopping place. It would not be, we knew, where we would raise our child.

The Levasseurs were living in their own house *à côte.* Their property abutted on Les Neiges. They were enormously proud of the whole and showed us details with delight: the linoleum pattern and wallpaper strips, the hot-water system and electrical *chauffage.* They had lived perforce without those aspects of modernity that we sought to escape; what represented status to them was what we took for granted, while we found discomfort, because temporary, charming. They had been surrounded by what we thought of as beauty, while its mismatched joinings and tendency to crumble drove them wild. Felicity in particular detested imprecision; she had scrubbed and polished the cracked tile floors of the old authentic *mas* and did not find them beautiful from her knee-high vantage. Guillaume had rather more a meditative and backward-glancing disposition; he wanted *des vieilles poutres,* old and worm-pocked beaming, as a design motif.

It is a law of design, I believe, and surely one of

architecture that anything more than one hundred years old acquires a dignified gloss. The most trivial of objects, provided it survives the twenty to fifty years when it seems merely outmoded, grows consequential then. And if there be a tourist one hundred years hereafter, he or she will wander in hushed admiration past our gas stations, cigarette dispensing machines, the Nissan and the Coca-Cola signs.

It's not, of course, that everything older is better. Many believe the reverse. I asked a mason once if he preferred to work with brick, stone, or cinder block. He had no college degree, no *nostalgie de la pierre.* He answered without hesitation that he liked cinder block best. I asked him why. "It makes a neater job."

Emblems from that time include Cesca in her stroller, transfixed by the foraging goats, or on Julia Child's table, eating chocolates, stuffing them into her mouth by fistfuls, then wiping her hands on her dress. On Elena's birthday a friend from Woodstock volunteered to baby-sit so we might have dinner in Mougins. The shock of separation was acute; we hurried home.

Plaster crumbled by the bath; there was mildew in the guest room; the cypress tree at the drive's crest was riven by a lightning storm; the stone retaining wall had buckled by the *cave.* "What are we doing here?" we asked each other daily. "What are we doing in this place? What do you think we should do?"

We continued to meet neighbors. There were veterans of the resistance, proud aging Jews with lame right legs or glass eyes. We met chemists and pianists and sailors and government officials whose government had changed. We met baronets with shopping bags and movie stars down on their luck. We met mystery writers and fashion designers and old soldiers dreaming of war. But none of it compelled attention as before; wave after wave of conquerors have washed up on the Esterel and then been washed away. The For Sale signs were everywhere, some of them written in English; the water tasted brackish, and the *moulin* sold souvenir oil.

That the traveler carries his personal luggage is by now not news. Of those who brought me first to France, my mother and Alex had died. Our daughter tottered, solitary, down the winding stair. Elena was not happy at the prospect of remaining in a stone house with poor plumbing, little heat, and long silent hours while I blackened the blank page. She had fewer illusions than I; she knew the French would treat us, however politely, as strangers—with a deep-seated wariness that could become contempt. Our visit was collective and familial and familiar; we would not stay the spring.

One reason was professional. I was a husband and father by then and well past thirty years old. Those authors who sustain careers as continual expatriates are few and far between. True exile is technically involuntary; many writers leave their native land because they cannot live there, or return. Early on, for instance, I asked Jimmy Baldwin what the title of his novel *Another Country* derived from, what was its original source. I thought perhaps he was making ironic reference to Hemingway's short story or to *The Jew of Malta* and Marlowe's famous phrase, "but that was in another country, and besides the wench is dead." It was, he told me, a Miltonic reference to a nettle that grows wild at home but that in another country would prove a valued flower.

Voluntary exile is a subtle, sapping thing; if Paris had been de rigueur for writers in the twenties, it had come to seem a bit beside the point. The point was, Jimmy said, to decide your subject and to see it steadily and whole. That might well prove impossible, but I should stop pretending to be rootless or a renegade. My first book had taken place in Greece, my most recent in the south of France, yet I voted in Vermont. He himself was planning to return. He would see us in New York.

A particular problem attaches to place—or does for this writer, at least. Once written of, it ceases to compel. If I see a detail I've included in a book, it seems less urgent to note; if I missed it earlier, I'm upset at the evident absence. No doubt many authors suffer this affliction—the sense that change connects to growth, the need to shift subjects as well as locale. Others, by contrast, dig more deeply with time or arrogate a single landscape as their own. Hardy or Faulkner would find the above a confession of weakness at best. But it is nonetheless the case that my attention wandered, that I started to write of New England instead and wanted to live where I wrote. The maxim has it that you know Paris in a week, feel uncertain in a year, and know after a decade that you know nothing at all.

It had been a dozen years since I first saw Les Neiges,

and change, though slow in coming, had to come. What powered me through adolescence and young manhood—the sense of willed apartness—felt less urgent now. I wanted to belong. They still tilled with horse-drawn plows between the rows of olives, still scythed the meadow by hand. But this was attitude, not necessity, and Guillaume preferred machines. When *la patronne* was out of town, he borrowed a neighbor's rototiller and roared through the forked rows.

We felt uselessly withdrawn from what was happening elsewhere and knew elsewhere was home. We returned the Deux Chevaux. The Levasseurs gave us, on our final day, a farewell party: crêpes, cold Provençal chicken, and wine in labeled bottles. This last was a gesture; we'd always shared *vin ordinaire*. When Guillaume drew the cork and flourished it, he acknowledged that he also knew we would not soon return.

XI

✳

1987

"Envoi: (F., 'a sending on the way.') Also *envoy*. A final stanza, shorter than the preceding ones, often used in the *ballade* and *chant royal* ... The *envoi* also repeats the refrain of the poem." So says *A Dictionary of Literary Terms*. There are several definitions in the *Oxford English Dictionary*. Here are two: "Now chiefly the short stanza which concludes a poem written in certain archaic metrical forms. *Arch*"; and "The conclusion of a play; also a catastrophe, denouement. *Obs.*"

So now, returning, in a rented beige Citroën BX16RS station wagon with Elena and two daughters and a mother's helper and much luggage, it has been eleven years. I had written Maija Bechstein and the Levasseurs. They were anxious and waiting to see us; they regretted that we could not all be neighbors once again.

Some years before, when fearful of declining health, Lilo Rosenthal had sold Les Neiges d'Antan. The new owner lived in Antibes. He maintained the property as an investment, not a home. Since Les Neiges was not available, they understood how we might choose to settle elsewhere; the Lubéron—or so wrote Guillaume—is "superb." Also, in the summer it is cool. And a quick visit is better than nothing, and they had reserved rooms in our name in Valbonne. The hotel was proper, Felicity assured me, she inspected the bedrooms herself. There was a swimming pool for the young ladies to enjoy; she could not express sufficiently her pleasure at the prospect of our reunion soon.

When I called Guillaume to confirm, however, he was guarded and *distrait.* Felicity was ill. He had just come from the hospital; we were lucky to find him at home. Perhaps I had tried earlier? He was spending all his time at the *clinique.* The crisis, however, had passed. Felicity was better, I could be assured of that; she hoped to be released in time for our arrival. The doctor would not promise but there was a chance. "Let's hope."

I asked him what had happened, and he was evasive: a blockage, a difficulty with the intestine, the small one, *heureusement.* She had been operated on last Thursday, that's why he wasn't at home. "The prognosis?" I inquired, and again he said, "Let's hope."

We drove east on the *autoroute,* coming from Aix-en-Provence. The stark shapes of the Esterel, the red rocks and apartments and vineyards and spires looked recognizable, not strange. Much of the surrounding hillside had been burned. The exit for Cannes/Le Cannet was the exit I had taken more than half my life before, following the map and then Alexander's instructions for Châteauneuf-de-Grasse. We needed no *Michelin* now. The road through Mougins was less private, perhaps, but the curves felt familiar, the banking unchanged; I knew when and where to shift gears. Each gas station, every restaurant or *tabac* or grocery store seemed an occasion for praise. "They're getting off on this," said Cesca. "They're heading down memory lane."

"They're really into it," Andrea said. "This is what you call a *trip!*"

They raised their thumbs; they slapped each other's hands. We checked into the small hotel, then drove to see Gourdon. Châteauneuf-de-Grasse and Pré-du-Lac were much as we remembered, and the trail incised in rock that leads up to the village will not alter till they learn to build a road on air. The valley of the Loup is steep and sheer. Gourdon perches on its outcrop like a bird alighting, stone talons curved into the cliff. The restaurant we hoped to visit was in fact called Le Nid d'Aigle, Eagle's Nest. The heat diminished as we climbed; there was a first faint breeze. The children were impressed. "Memory lane," I told them. "I used to do this in the winter."

"Don't have wine for lunch," Andrea said. "OK?"

"I can drive it with my eyes closed."

"Don't," she said.

We parked in the flat field beneath the village; access is on foot. The field was full of cars. We were part of a sightseeing legion—Sunday couples with toddlers or a baby carriage, boys with backpacks and knee socks and hiking boots, men with flowered shirts and pocketbooks, elderly ladies with canes. There were Germans, Italians, and Danes; there were thin women in dresses and thick ones wearing shorts. We joined them and marched up the hill.

It is difficult to know, in this century of Heisenberg and Einstein, what is absolute, what relative, and why. Do we change as witnesses, or does that which we witness change, or both; does it alter because of the viewing, and is our estimate altered by the very consciousness of sight? These problems of philosophy and mathematics are domestic riddles also; was it *always* just like this, and did we fail to notice? The Abbaye de Thoronet, for example, looked the same. We had stopped there, driving east. The Cistercian rock pile was being shored up by the government, and the restoration effort appeared to be advancing at the same rate as collapse. But what had seemed impressive once was merely shabby now; the great arching silent structure seemed more an engineering problem than an act of faith.

Further, I had known Gourdon in every season but summer—and summer is the season for the tourist trade. So those shuttered stone houses and empty echoing streets may have been misleading—or a part of the truth—even then. Now the doorways were open, the shutters ajar; inside they sold perfumes and postcards and honey and film and cassettes and T-shirts and toilet water and pottery and soap. A bouquet of herbes de Provence cost precisely three times what we had paid the day before in the Saturday market at Apt.

And Le Nid d'Aigle was closed. It had been closed, we learned, for years. From the small square at the village crest you could see its empty terrace, see a blue hang glider off by Bar-sur-Loup. The telescope remained, and the plane trees giving shade. The heat-haze in the valley made the long view less spectacular, but the middle distance—hills scumbled with thyme, the stunted pine, the boulders stacked for shipment at a quarry's rim—acquired definition. We ate at the remaining restaurant instead.

The Taverne Provençal was chock-a-block with customers; we found a table on the patio at half past two. I had delivered gas here, with Guillaume, when the paving was ice-slick. The *patron* who gave us coffee in 1964 was, his successor told me, dead—or possibly retired. The waiter was not sure. The waiter was busy and young and would not have wished to reminisce about winters before he was born. *La recherche du temps perdu* is a sentimental enterprise, and sentiment requires leisure, and leisure is expensive. He would sit and reminisce, perhaps, in twenty years, or in the autumn, or when the table was cleared. Till then, the question was, did I want another bottle of Tavel?

The girls said no. They bought all-day suckers; they visited the "History-of-Perfume Source," and we careened back down. "The eagle has landed," Elena announced. "We made it, after all."

"What time is it back home?" Andrea asked. "Shouldn't we be eating breakfast?"

"I'm looking forward," Cesca said, "to looking back on this."

We drove through Opio and then—intending to pretend we were lost, were strangers, were simply at the driveway's crest intending to turn back again—up to Les Neiges d'Antan. Its signpost remained.

The driveway was pitted, the gravel washed free. Weeds flourished at the curb. The beds of lavender and lilies that had served as border, those roses that punctured the NSU Prinz, were grass-choked now, a thicket. The olive trees grew wild. The peach orchard had been wrecked. I could see all this while bumping up the ruts; it took no skill to see. Adam's garden was a tangle now, the gardeners dismissed.

Guard dogs met us at the driveway's crest. The larger one seemed savage, and his small piebald companion made noise. We turned around. They followed us, descending, to the lightning-stunted cyprus; the fig tree and the oaks behind the house were gone. I could see this, shifting gears. Later I would hear, from an outraged implacable Guillaume, that the new owner from Antibes had massacred the oaks. *"Le massacre des chênes,"* he called it, and the fig tree also; one day a team drives up with saws, for no adequate reason, for nothing at all. Dirk Bogarde had been shocked. He was not here any longer, Guillaume explained, but he made a particular point of commiserating with the Levasseurs. "I never hope to see *un tel atroce* again," said Guillaume. "Such an atrocity. In order to improve *le parking.* Imagine, those beautiful trees. And the mimosa froze. I tell you, Nicholas, *ce type* has much to answer for. He's mad, he wants only money, he thought he would improve the view but it is inexcusable. The oaks."

Shaken, we drove to the Levasseur house. *This* one was well tended, and Guillaume waited in the doorway, arms held out. His hair was gray, and he might have gained five pounds, but he appeared unchanged: wiry, high-voiced, courteous, embracing Elena who dwarfed him, greeting Cesca whom he last had seen in diapers and who was now his size, shaking Andrea's hand and telling her she looked exactly like—no, more lovely than—her photographs. He told me that I had not aged, and I denied it, and he denied my denial; we beat each other on the back and kissed each other's cheeks. "How is Felicity?" we asked, and he said, "Better. Much better than this morning. The doctor gives us no reason to worry, he says she's better at home."

She was sitting in a corner on the porch. She tried to stand. We told her not to, and she stood up, wincing. "It's brave of you," Elena said.

"It's stupid," said Felicity. "I have been stupid all my life." She smiled. "That does not change."

We drank champagne. Guillaume feared it was not cold enough, and Felicity said how much better this champagne would have tasted if cold. We praised its perfect chill and offered presents and spread out maps to prove that Michigan existed; we asked after family, neighbors and friends. The chain saw that Elena's father had given Guillaume fifteen years before still worked. "It works so well in fact," he said, "I lend it out. *Mon Dieu,* the wood it has cut!" He flapped his hand, loose-wristed. *"Que de bois!"*

Andrea found a pair of caged birds nesting. He said, "They adore each other. They share this nest. They sing. They were singing before you arrived."

We spoke of who had died and who retired in the village—the postmistress, the butcher, the mayor, the English painter up the hill, and, last year, Lady B. I asked to see his garden; he demurred. "It's a disgrace, this garden.

Ce n'est pas beau. I've been in the *clinique* all week, you understand, and before that we were visiting in Château-roux."

The tenants at Les Neiges had gone away for the week. They were good *locataires,* kind people, decent and respectable; he had no complaints about them but only disdain for the owner. Those who rented would not mind if we took a quick look; he had the key. He would show the children where we used to live.

We went in through the *cave.* The kitchen had been changed. *"Vous allez voir,* Nicholas, it's much more convenient, they heat it now with gas." As always, I had asked him to use the less formal mode of address, *tu,* not the respectful *vous;* as always, he declined. But Guillaume was delighted, enumerating the improvements made by his friends the *locataires;* he ticked them off on his fingers. *"Moins cher, moins de travail, moins sale."* That it was less expensive, less work, and less dirty meant nothing to me; nor did the improvements in the stove. The old stone sink had been replaced, the breadbox taken off the wall, the doorway masked with a fake plaster arch. The banquette in the dining room was gone, and a kitchenette inserted on the facing wall.

It was better, no doubt, but all wrong. The tenants had had a free hand. Monsieur from Antibes was selling off the olive groves for building sites, since that was where his profit lay, and the little house meant nothing to him so he let the renters arrange things for their comfort. Happily, said Guillaume, they loved the house; the fireplace was working. And often and often he thought of me, how content I would have been those winters with a fireplace. Monsieur Piasco the mason and he had unbricked the chimney after the oak massacre, and—he raised his hand, astonished—*voilà,* it functions now.

The furniture was cheap. Upstairs, the beds were gone. The guest room with its pallet and sink, its chair and desk and aspect of van Gogh in his coruscating madness, now held twin beds from motels. The master bedroom had a double bed; the armoire had been ripped from the hall. The pull-chain toilet and the upright bathtub, too, were gone; modern plumbing fixtures had been inserted instead. It looked not unlike the hairdresser's house from which we fled in Châteauneuf-de-Grasse.

"It's nice in here," Andrea said.

"Yes."

"Except we wouldn't fit. Not four of us."

"This was the window," said Elena. "Where you could see Corsica."

"I know a joke," said Cesca. "Pretend you're the teacher. And then ask me if I know what nationality Napoleon had when he was born."

"All right," I said. "Can you tell me, students, what nationality Napoleon had when he was born?"

"Cors-I-can," she said. "Get it? Corsican."

"You couldn't really see it," said Elena. "But you could see its reflection."

"We must go." Guillaume conducted us back down the stairs. *"On s'en va."*

The meadow had been mowed. There where the wild-flowers flourished was machine-cut grass. All else was wreckage, proof of poor tending or loss to the worms and the ice. The dogs were chained. We took our leave. Felicity was resting. She would feel better tomorrow, she promised, she would see us in the morning and we mustn't mind. Guillaume would be sixty-five next month; she wanted to be ready for the *fête.* "The little house," she said. "It's not the way it was before. But nothing is."

I could not tell her—could not phrase it even to myself just then—that, far from disappointed, I was relieved. Had the space been splendid, as roseate as memory, I would have mourned our absence, our elected distance; now it simply seemed like some other someone's shelter, the roof for strangers' heads. Long after Adam took his leave—so Malcolm Lowry wrote—the light in his house continued to burn. Someone else says, "Say, here's Eden," and fixes the paint job and carpets the floor. They call it Dunroamin; they buy a better mattress and a microwave. It is an exile from nothing, a private not a public fall, a problem with the apple harvest since the original worm.

We drove the ten minutes to Magagnosc and descended to La Lauve. We parked above the Bechstein house and made our way past children, men in undershirts, women folding laundry off the line. We knocked. There was no answer. The house presents, as do most other village houses, a cold closed-forward face. Its shutters were fastened; it might have been empty; the tax assessor cannot gauge, from an exterior survey, the wealth of the household within. (In America this situation, and the value system that engenders it, seems the reverse. One can admire beautifully maintained facades of houses in New England, where there is no plumbing and only a dirt floor. If a farmer has the time and money to paint just one side of his barn, he paints the side fronting the road. But in the south of France—in Mediterranean countries throughout—you cannot tell a household by its cover; the courtyard or the rear facade will show you far more than the street.)

Maija was in her garden. Finally she heard my knock; we went around the wall. She limped. We had last seen her three years previous, on a visit she paid to New York. She was seventy years old. But her aspect was girlishly glad; she trilled and warbled out hello; she kissed Elena, then the girls, pronouncing their full names. "Andrea Katherine Delbanco. Francesca Barbara Delbanco. What pleasure to see you again."

She had been at Magagnosc since April and without a car. She was leaving for Switzerland soon. She had grandchildren now, and it was difficult to be without them for so long. "You know," she turned to me, "when Alex died it was all over. For seven years it was finished, I had no reason to go on. I just went on because there was also no reason to stop. But then, when my grandson was born"—she smiled—"well, I started living again."

"He would have been delighted."

"Yes."

Her accent was thick, English slow. We spoke in an amalgam of English and German and French. She told us that her love of matters French was fading, that she missed Switzerland now. The town of Grasse was a horror, she said; she went there once a week, and only to the Monoprix. They do not wash their fruit or vegetables anymore; the perfumes are synthetic since they sold off all the flowers to make space for the construction, *afin de construire.* And everyone is lazy now and there is no one to trust. You pay for work and they don't do it, or you have to watch continually; you pay in advance and nothing gets done; you don't pay in advance and they fail to arrive, *c'est affreux.* Last year she fell and hurt her knee and the French doctors wished to operate, but she called her doctor also in Berne. She had given money to the medical emergency *équipe* in Berne— you know, those helicopter teams that rescue people from the mountains. So they rescued her. It was the best hundred francs she had ever invested for charity; she had become, she laughed, the charity herself. They sent two nurses and an ambulance from Nice. It had been her seventieth birthday, and the nurses, knowing that, brought along flowers and chocolate. Then there was a helicopter waiting to fly her to Zurich, then another ambulance to Berne. And the Swiss doctors were waiting, and they said we daren't operate; we are skilled at this procedure—more skilled, perhaps, although it is boastful to say so, than the veterinarian in Grasse—but it's too delicate for certainty, it will instead heal by itself. The knee did heal. It hurt, of course, but healed.

Her house was three small houses, linked, with a garden for the fourth wall. Two of these were homes she occupied with Alex, the third a *pigeonnier.* He had completed the first when he died and had drawn up the plans for the vaulted music room that was to hold her piano. They had contracted with the mason for the work. So she went ahead with renovation, scrupulously following his sketches for her wedding gift: the way the two front-facing houses would connect, the bathroom underneath the stairs, the platform for the piano that meant, playing, she could also have the view. This took two years.

She could not, however, bring herself to play. She knew what the music should sound like, but her fingers could no longer make it happen. She listened to Schubert instead. Alfred Brendel playing Schubert was sufficient reason to stop fumbling at the piano by herself. So she sold the piano and put up the front houses for sale. They were too much. They reminded her, continually, of Alex, and her knee would not grow supple, and there were too many stairs.

She was working on the *pigeonnier* instead. That was enough. There was a garden to work on and one little room with a view, and her children could come to the pigeon house, and her grandchildren when they were old enough to travel. She was boring our daughters, she knew. She had bought potato chips and Coca-Cola for them; Americans like ice. "You"—she turned to me—"you're still a European, partly, but no doubt you also want ice."

We sat beneath the fig tree. It grew dark. Planes angled down the last line of light at the edge of the water, making for Nice. "It's beautiful," Elena said.

"You think so?" Maija said. "But there is so much building, so many trucks."

"Not in your garden."

"No. But it's a kind of horror when I have to go

to Grasse." She smiled again. "One old lady walking."
"It's difficult," I said. "It must be hard."
"Either you finish or you start. And both of those are simple. The hardest thing is to continue. That's what I find hard."

Early next morning we traveled to Cannes. At eight o'clock it still proved possible to find a parking space; the Croisette had been sluiced down and cleaned. We walked down past the Carleton Hotel to the sea. The umbrellas for the Carleton beach were not yet open, the pillows still stacked. A blackboard promised spectacular fireworks for the celebration tomorrow; for 250 francs you could reserve a place. It was advisable to reserve in advance; the fireworks would be superb. The heat increased. An American battleship lay at anchor out by the Iles de Lerins; a girl in a bikini bottom was water-skiing. She flashed and swooped and shifted weight; the motorboat was planing, and it roared. She waved it out towards the ship, to entertain the troops. They would be entertained. The shore patrol, walking in threes, their black shoes shining, whites brilliant in the brilliant light, eyes right, secured the beach.

The morning was beginning on the rue d'Antibes. The first shops were opening, the salesgirls raising canopies, the *tabac* dispensing magazines and packs of cigarettes. The hairdressers and tanning salons and tea rooms would open at nine. One girl held up a cascade of brown hair with her right hand; she worked doubled over, swiping at the letters of the storefront—*Emaux et Camées*—with a sponge. She did this facing the street.

On the Croisette, however, the jewelers and the galleries would not prepare for business till ten. We took off our shoes and advanced to the shoreline; the beach was occupied. It belonged to the elderly, early; they would be displaced. But the bronzed youth of Cannes, and those who paid to join them, were still asleep at this hour—some perhaps going to sleep. An old man with a bright blue skullcap and bikini brief, skin the color of walnuts, scuttled past with coffee in a plastic cup. Nursemaids read their newspapers on blue folding chairs. Couples watched their children and grandchildren kicking sand; a very fat woman took off her bathing suit top and took a shower from the public spigot up against the sea wall. She bounced and sang and shimmied, using soap. A blind bearded man swept his cane on the sand; men smoked and rubbed themselves with oil and tested the backs of their legs. The water was briny and hot. This congregation knew intruders; they did not smile or speak to us. We were standing in their sun.

Grasse, that perfumed village, stank of exhaust fumes and strained septic systems and cats. It was hard to find a parking place, hard to dismiss the throb of commerce—bulldozers, cranes wheeling and grinding above the apartments, fliers everywhere from Molinard and Gallimard and Fragonard, urging the tourist to visit the factory, to "initiate yourself in the secrets of perfume." They ballyhooed the "sym-

phony of aromas which give character to the great perfumes"; they promised that "Our hostesses will welcome
you in your own language."

Cesca bought lipstick, Elena perfume. Then we left.
Once more we drove to Opio; Felicity felt better. She sat
in the same corner of the porch, blanket-swaddled, but the
old animation was with her. She had had a bath. We told
her what had happened to Elena in the hotel bath; first she
seemed shocked, then she laughed. When I said she would
play *boules* again, she said, *"Tireur et pointeur!* I am ready for
you now."

Guillaume had been working in the garden; this
time he let me see. "I work a little bit," he said. "Just
enough for us, so that we have what's necessary. I'm not
proud of it, you understand, but it does provide. There are
those who spend their time entirely in gardens; I'm not such
a type. I worked every day of my life from the day I was
sixteen. And I don't want to be a slave again to anything,
you understand, not even to a garden. It can enslave you
like work."

The descent to his garden was steep. "I get my exercise"—he smiled—"just running up and down this hill. I
ought to put in stairs." He was wearing his blue slippers
with the rubber soles.

My soles were slick. I held to the fig tree, then peach
tree, descending. Underneath the fruit trees, the olive trees
began. "I have had them pruned," he said. His land had
been terraced, the soil a thick orange clay. There was lettuce; there were rows of beans. We talked about the quality
of vegetables in the Lubéron and gardening in the Dordogne. He too had seen the caves. He knelt approvingly.

"This year the beans are good. And every year is good for onions. Onions and garlic are at home here, *dans le Midi.* I have winter onions up above, but these are the white onions for just now." They were drying in clumps, firm and full. We discussed the growing time for his eggplant and tomatoes, as opposed to my own in Vermont. He would have tomatoes in two weeks. *"Que j'ai cueilli des pêches,"* he said. "The peaches I had here last year."

Then we came to raspberries. "We should have brought your daughters down," said Guillaume. "I said to myself, they would like to pick berries, they would enjoy them so ripe." We picked a handful and ate them warm. I continued eating, while he collected berries for those waiting on the porch. It was, of a sudden, standing there—the sky bright blue, the silvery olives beneath us, the soft wind and the perfect fruit—as if there were no damage: no one had died, no one was ill or aging or corrupt. "I very much esteem," he said, "that you could come to visit."

We made our way back to the house.